THE FIG TREE BLOSSOMS

MESSIANIC JUDAISM EMERGES

by Paul Liberman

DEDICATION

To Susan, who also understands.

Distributed by:
International Messianic Jewish Alliance
72-877 Dinah Shore Drive
Suite 103-141
Rancho Mirage, CA 92270

Reprint 1977
Reprint 1980
Reprint 1982 (Hebrew translation)
Reprint 1983 (Hebrew translation)
Reprint 1987
Reprint 1988
Reprint 1989
Reprint 1992
Reprint 1994
Reprint 1995 (Hebrew translation)
Reprint 1997
Reprint 1997 (Russian translation)
Reprint 2001
Reprint 2005

Published by Fountain Press, Indianola, Iowa 50125.
Printed in the United States of America.
I.S.B.N.: 0-89350-0003

TABLE OF CONTENTS

PREFACE

The sudden surge in the number of Jews recognizing the Messiah of Israel has created a stir in the traditional Jewish community. It also has been the source of much excitement among true believers in the Messiah. During the first century, Messianic believers were practically all Jewish. Messianic Judaism flourished during the next 300 years, then laid virtually dormant until the Arab-Israeli Six Day War in 1967.

The end of that war was the beginning of a greater Jewish consciousness among Jews themselves, and it has swept across nations. It also marked the time when Jews who accepted the New Testament no longer wished to be absorbed into traditional church institutions. Such Jews preferred to be called Messianic Jews. This is a departure from the past, but it does not represent any biblical inconsistency. In recent years this desire to maintain a Jewish identification has intensified.

If 1967 was the birthdate of modern Messianic Judaism, then 1975 was the year the movement officially began to blossom. For some decades, Jewish believers in the Messiah were content to be trophies on the shelf of traditional church institutions. Today this is no longer the case. The new Jew, armed with the truth, has the burden of bringing the Messianic message to other Jews throughout the world.

In mid-1975, about 600 Messianic Jews met at a national

conference called Messiah '75. There, leaders from all over the United States, Europe and Israel discussed the role of Messianic Jews in relation to traditional Judaism.

It became apparent during the conference that the story of Messianic Judaism needed to be told in clear, uncomplicated language. Up until then, dozens of books had been written on related subjects. None of them, however, comprehensively explained what the movement was all about.

It also has become obvious that events are moving rapidly and theologians will be investigating and dissecting this new phenomenon for years. In the meantime, it seems necessary to present a broad brush panorama of these new and exciting developments.

To be sure, this book is not intended as a deep theological treatise. Rather, it brings together many current thoughts of the thousands of Messianic Jews throughout this nation.

This is not to say that the movement lacks scholarship. Indeed, Messiah '75, among other things, showcased a wealth of theological talent. The many lectures given during this week-long conference attest to this. They were extremely helpful in the preparation of this book.

One lecture especially worthy of mention was given by Arnold Fruchtenbaum. Much of Chapter IV of this book, Early Messianic Jewish History, has been based upon his presentation.

Many of the other chapters express thoughts or facts that are common knowledge among Messianic Jews. They are offered here, hoping to provide fresh insight for believers in the Messiah and for those who have not yet accepted the Messianic fulfillment.

Much of the terminology used herein emphasizes the Jewishness of the New Testament. In a similar vein, every scriptural quotation is from the Harkavy edition of the Jewish Bible published by the Hebrew Publishing Co.

"I found Israel like grapes in the wilderness; I saw your fathers as the first-ripe in the fig tree."

Hosea 9:10

I

MESSIANIC JUDAISM: AN OVERVIEW

It traditionally has been accepted that Judaism and Christianity are separate and distinct. This belief is being challenged by a new and growing number of Jewish people who accept both the Old and New Testaments as valid. For such Jews, the long-expected Messiah has come. These Messianic Jews are experiencing a personal relationship with the God of Abraham, Isaac and Jacob. Historically, whenever a Jew accepted the New Testament, he was rejected by his own family and friends as a turncoat and traitor. He was severed from his people and considered a Gentile. Conversely, the Christian church accepted the new believer and told him in subtle ways he no longer was Jewish. He was accepted as a member of the church and the issue seemed clear-cut from the viewpoint of both Jewish and Christian institutions.

Although both groups saw these philosophies as distinctly different, the issues were more difficult for the individuals involved, or for their families. There was little reason for these families to investigate the precepts on which this change of heart was based. The personal trauma usually was so severe, the stigma so great, the new believer was glad for the refuge of his new church rather than suffer continual rebuke from his former synagogue and personal acquaintances. How comfortable for everyone concerned except the new Jewish believer! The rebuke he was to suffer usually included disdain from his family and friends and, in some cases, he was written off with a funeral service.

For nearly 2,000 years, the Christian church has not fulfilled its mission to bring the good news of the coming of the Messiah to the world's Jewish population. The time for change has come.

A tenet of Messianic Judaism asserts that when a Jew accepts a Jewish Messiah, born in a Jewish land, who was foretold by Jewish prophets in the Jewish Scriptures, such a Jew does not become a Gentile. In fact, he becomes a completed Jew—a Jew who believes Jesus is the Messiah. This is because he not only has the promise of a Messiah, he actually knows Him. Where ritual and tradition previously were obligatory, they now take on a higher meaning. They are seen as the foreshadowing of God's overall plan. Such traditions now give a Jew a sense of purpose and a link with his cultural past.

Messianic Judaism is not a new cult seeking to separate itself from the body of believers in the Messiah. It is a way of reconciling belief in the Messiah while continuing to be a Jew. This is important when attempting to explain about the Messiah to traditional Jews. Who else can better be a Jew to Jews?

By becoming better Jews, by being interested in Hebrew Scriptures and the State of Israel, traditional Judaism no longer can justify the claim that acceptance of the New Testament is an attempt by other Jews to assimilate. Also, by speaking in a united voice, the full chorus of such transformed lives can be heard. This adds credibility to Jewish believers in the New Covenant, and checks efforts to write them off as a few misguided fanatics.

The reason the institutional church has been so unsuccessful in bringing the good news of the Messiah to the Jewish people is tied to its failure to recognize an element of Jewish psychology. Every Jew, no matter how irreligious, knows he was born a Jew and wants to die a Jew. Any concept which threatens that view is bound to fail. Unwittingly, the institutional church has erred by insisting that Jews give up their identification. There is nothing in the Scriptures that requires Jews to stop being Jews when they accept the Messiah.

As a matter of fact, the Scriptures strongly support the concept that Jews remain Jews, after they come to know their Lord personally. Early followers of the Messiah continued going to synagogues and celebrating festivals as they always had done. Saul of Tarsus, after changing his name to Paul, spoke of himself as a Jew. He did not refer to himself as a former Jew and he underwent the purification required by festival procedures.

Moreover, Paul instructed Timothy to be circumcised to affirm his Judaism. Any true believer in the Lord realizes that outward forms of expression are secondary to obtaining an inner peace in this life and eternal rest in the hereafter. This true peace is available to anyone who openly looks at the truth.

Another point of confusion is that Jewish people assume that all non-Jews of western culture are Christians. Since they are Jewish from birth, they assume one becomes a Christian the same way. Most Jews do not understand that many people go to church and masquerade as Christians, but lack the supernatural awakening necessary to become true followers of the Messiah. Since Jewish people are unable to make such a distinction, they take it for granted that all who attend church are believers in the New Covenant. They assume that spiritual viewpoints are determined according to what family a person is born into. It seldom occurs to traditional Jews that it is possible to have a personal encounter with God.

Once it is recognized that Jewish people lump together

all those under the Catholic and Protestant institutional umbrellas, it is easier to understand why symbols, such as the cross, are distasteful and oppressive to them. Inquisitions, holocausts and social discrimination reinforce their view.

Before Jews can distinguish between true believers and nominal church members, they must have had a personal encounter with God. Yet how can they obtain such experience if believing Gentiles constantly confront them with alien symbols which prevent them from giving the New Covenant fair evaluation? In order to get a fair hearing, it is reasonable to expect the believer to go out of his way to avoid offending Jewish people. Remember, for almost 2,000 years these church symbols have only driven Jewish people further from their God.

The Messianic Jew directs his efforts toward removing these obstacles. He has a built-in incentive to do so. His family and friends haven't gotten into God's program yet. So he carefully tries to remove roadblocks to understanding. For this reason, discussion emphasizes the scriptural Jewishness of these seemingly Gentile concepts.

For example, the name Jesus Christ generally is a bone in the throat of Jewish people. This is because so much wrong has been done in His name by those who affiliate with a church, but who have no knowledge of God. Since it creates a problem for Jewish people, why not call Jesus by his Hebrew name, Yeshua Ha Mashiach? This in no way indicates shame of His name, it simply removes a linguistic obstacle. Besides, the Hebrew name Yeshua Ha Mashiach is more technically correct. When followers saw the carpenter from Galilee they didn't say, "There goes Jesus Christ." They spoke Hebrew and Aramaic and probably referred to Him by His given name and title. When His Hebrew name was translated into Greek, it became Hesus Christos (Haysoos Kres-tos). This was later anglicized to "Jesus Christ."

The literal translation of Yeshua is "Salvation," and Ha Mashiach means "the Messiah" (the anointed one). Thus, Jesus Christ literally means "Salvation is of the Messiah." Isn't it much more reasonable and more palatable to speak Hebrew when talking to a Hebrew?

This explanation also may help clarify the term "Messianic Jew." Since the word "Christian" comes from the Hebrew word meaning Messiah, why not call a Christian Jew a Messianic Jew?

Here are some other language substitutes generally less offensive to traditional Jews:

Suggested	Avoid
Messiah Yeshua	Christ Jesus
Become a "completed Jew"	Convert
A Bible believer	Christian
Second part of the Bible or New Covenant	New Testament

Beyond semantical differences, the Bible clearly portrays Jews as a distinctive people. Even when a Jew is completed and becomes a part of the body of the Messiah, he still has a distinctive function. Each part of the body has a different task. If God didn't want Jews preserved as a distinctive people for a reason, He certainly wouldn't have gone to the trouble to do so. What God has gone to so much trouble to preserve, what child of God would dare tamper with it? The great role of the Jewish people was to bring the Messiah and the Word of God to the peoples of the world; it still is. Hebrews were chosen to be a holy people. God called them the apple of His eye.

The Lord is using Messianic Judaism for another purpose. He is using it to break down what the Bible refers to as a middle wall of partition between Jew and Gentile which has existed for so many centuries.

Messianic Judaism is living proof there is no essential difference between Christianity and the true Judaism of the Bible. Thus, the existence of completed Jews forces the fair-minded traditional Jew to examine his criteria for determining what a Jew is. If he is honest with himself, he will admit that in today's context a Jew can be a philosopher, academic, dope addict, sex pervert, alcoholic, atheist or a ne'er-do-well and still be identified as a Jew. This is true even if he has never been to a synagogue.

Yet, if a person of Jewish parentage reads the Old Testament daily, speaks Hebrew, is wholesome and believes in Yeshua, Rabbis would have us believe this person is no longer part of the great Jewish heritage. Because of this baseless belief, Jews are being forced to redefine their Jewishness. In an honest search of Old Testament Scriptures, a Jew must eventually concede it was faith in God's Word which distinguished his ancestral patriarchs.

In all other matters, Jews have welcomed truth regardless of its source. Knowledge has been accepted from Aristotle, Plato, Homer, Milton and so on, but there is one name—Yeshua—that traditional Jews draw the line on. What has He done wrong, and why is His wisdom not even worthy of investigation? After all, He has changed so many lives, been the focus of a great religion and drawn praise from the multitudes. Why shouldn't doctrines so completely consistent with Jewish Scriptures be accepted by His fellow Jews?

Today's enlightened Jews have ceased blaming this man of Galilee for atrocities committed by pagans falsely called Christians. True Judaism today recognizes Yeshua as one of their own. Although many others have been self-proclaimed

Messiahs, one is hard pressed to remember their names. Military leaders like Alexander, Caesar and Napoleon, even a little corporal named Hitler—have sought to conquer the world, and all ended in failure.

Only one can claim to have captured the hearts of so many. He has not done it by might or power, but by the Spirit of God. Today, as in the first century, the Jew is asked: "What do you think of this man Yeshua?" As it always has been, some accept Him, others reject Him. The Messiah wasn't meant for one generation, but for all generations. For some people the Messiah has arrived; for others He has not become apparent. He only has come to people who believe God's Word.

When we look at history, it is almost as if the organized church and synagogues have been eager to persuade the world that believers of the New Covenant are something apart from their Jewish foundations. As a matter of fact, one cannot fully understand the Christian faith apart from its foundations. This alone should destroy the mistaken concept that true Judaism and true Christianity are opposed to one another. Christian faith depends upon the Jewish Bible. Even the New Covenant was written by Jews. The only possible exception would be the Book of Luke, since his ethnic origin is not definitely known. Yeshua Himself was a Jew; so were His twelve disciples. The first Christian community was all-Jewish, and the first great teacher of the Gentiles, Paul, was Jewish. Today's Messianic Jews simply are picking up where their first century ancestors left off.

Greek, or western orientation, is what makes the Christian faith so foreign to Jewish people. The original theology—its concepts and ideas—can best be comprehended in the Hebrew lingual context, and in the context of Jewish history. Even the New Covenant makes it explicit that all who believe in the Messiah are "children of Abraham" by faith. Paul called them "true Israel." According to Paul, through whom the Gentile world was to receive the good news that Yeshua is the Messiah, a Gentile becomes a proselyte to biblical Judaism when he accepts the faith of Abraham. This may seem somewhat paradoxical, since there are so many more Christians than Jews. But God is unimpressed by numerical superiority. From His viewpoint, the New Covenant really is a continuation of the Old Testament. It is amazing to consider how distorted our thinking has become over the ages. But God had a purpose in permitting this.

The Almighty didn't plan to give His Message to a small group of Semitic people in one corner of the world. A fair and merciful God wouldn't leave all the rest of mankind to be excluded from a relationship with Him. It is interesting to speculate whether this would have happened had Jews accepted Yeshua as Messiah.

Gentiles have an obligation toward Jews for having given them God's Word. According to the New Covenant, the Jewish people will receive God's Word through the mercy of the Gentiles.

Then Jews will be grateful to Gentiles, and neither will be at the other's disadvantage. Each group will appreciate the other. In this way, God will make all men brothers. Only a fair and just God could devise such a plan.

The survival of the Jewish people is the best evidence of the Bible's validity. What other people, so small in number, have endured so long despite the most adverse circumstances? God easily could have snuffed out a people with so little to recommend. But God must keep His promise to Abraham's seed. Since the biblical prophecy is for the Jew to survive despite all adversity, it is reasonable to assume that God had a purpose for their preservation. If Jews did not survive, how could God deliver on His promises to Abraham, Isaac and Jacob? The Jew is an enduring memorial to the validity of God's Holy Word.

Why, then, do Gentile believers in the Messiah want Jews to stop being Jews when they accept their Jewish Messiah? It isn't consistent with Scripture for Jews to give up their ancient heritage. This desire to continue to be Jewish is what has kept Jewish people a viable and distinctive group through the ages. If there no longer were any recognizable Jewish people, how could God keep His promise to Abraham concerning the land of Israel? What point would there be in worshipping a God who doesn't keep His Word?

God's adversary, Satan, fully realizes the importance of the Jewish people to God's plan. That's why Satan always has sought to promote anti-Semitism. The devil realizes that if he can destroy these ancient people, he will have successfully challenged the Lord who promised that the Jewish people would endure.

No other group can claim to have people who are descendents of the twelve tribes fathered by Jacob. Isn't it reasonable, then that if there is to be a world evangelization by these twelve tribes, as the Bible predicts, they should be identified as Jews?

Some well-meaning believers take a legalistic posture and are against change of any kind. As with any Scripture, if it is interpreted too legalistically, its underlying meaning becomes obscure. Didn't Messiah Yeshua advocate change in the Temple's operation and in mankind's view of God? Didn't Paul advocate change by which Gentiles would not have to become Jewish in order to accept the Messiah?

Paul was a radical. He said Gentiles did not have to accept Jewish ceremonies. He maintained that the important thing was the condition of the heart. Now the situation is reversed. The Gentile believers are the establishment, which have their own modes of worship. Paul probably would argue today that the state of Jewish hearts should be of primary concern, and symbols and rituals are of secondary importance.

Time has shown the wisdom of this viewpoint. Time also will decide the wisdom of letting Jews remain Jews.

A question along these lines was put to the great sage Gamaliel. As the leading scholar of first century Israel, he was asked about the Messianic movement surrounding the carpenter from Galilee and His miracles. People wanted to know whether Yeshua was sponsored by God or Satan. Gamaliel said if He was sent by God, nothing anyone did would prevent this movement from being established. If he wasn't, the movement would dissolve on its own. The early Messianic movement was God's will and it was established. This was the acid test, and it likewise will be for modern Messianic Judaism.

Wisdom such as this did not depend upon man's opinion. Dedicated Jewish scholars sought to give commentary about the Scriptures over many centuries. Their views were organized and compiled into what is known as the Talmud, the Midrash and the Mishna.

There was nothing wrong with men exchanging views about God's Scriptures. Much of the study was quite interesting. Unfortunately, Jewish scholars became so involved with the book reviews, they tended to minimize the importance of the Book itself. In time, there was little or no distinction made between what was scriptural and what was rabbinical opinion. Eventually, these writings largely became the basis for the development of Jewish practices. In effect, much of what is modern-day traditional Judaism is really misnamed. It should be referred to as belief in Rabbi's opinions (Rabbinism).

Most advocates of traditional Judaism are unaware of how much their practices come from rabbinical commentary, rather than from biblical commandment. The organized church also has indulged in the same sort of rule making. Just like the rabbinical writings, they have been well-intentioned and often have the force of law within the denomination.

Having been victimized by the distortions of Scripture, Messianic Jews are quick to make a distinction between Scripture and scholarly opinion. While scholarship is necessary, it should not carry the spiritual authority of Scripture. Above all, when scholarly opinion is in conflict with Scripture, it should be recognized as a well-intentioned error.

The Messianic Jew accepts the Word of God and its content as the basis for his beliefs. The Scriptures are the Jews' title deed to the land of Israel, to the survival of the Jewish people, and the guarantee of God's eternal covenant.

It is a basic tenet of Messianic Judaism that the Old and New Testaments were inspired by God, and they really are one message. There are no precepts in the New Covenant which contradict the Old Testament. Since Messianic Judaism rests so heavily upon the Bible, perhaps it is useful to examine some of the reasons for this.

II
THE BIBLE IS TRUE

Other than nature's handiwork, there probably is no greater evidence of the existence of an almighty God than the Bible. Skeptics quickly suggest that the Scriptures were handed down over many generations and they are the product of myth and exaggeration.

Precisely because these holy words have been preserved for so long, credence is given to the ageless claim that the Bible was supernaturally inspired. How many other stories have lasted so long, offer so much detail, and seem so consistent with mankind's performance?

Secular history supports the timing of events described in this great document. Imagine how aware of past and present events an author—or any combination of authors—would have to be to write such a detailed account. When you consider the Bible's infinite detail about people, customs and events, it becomes clear that its message was written by inspired men who either lived during biblical days, or recounted historical events with uncanny accuracy.

If these were false reports, why were the scriptural writings considered authentic by others living in the same era? Many of these events concerned kings, nations and large numbers of ordinary people. If these works were not accurate, others would have quickly provided contrary evidence. This would be particularly true considering that the events took place in a land virtually obsessed with religion.

Discovery of the Dead Sea Scrolls provide more tangible evidence of the Holy Scriptures' authenticity. These writings were completed before the time of Yeshua by members of an Essene sect. They are amazingly identical to the Scriptures we read today. Although the Scrolls are not conveniently separated into chapters and verses like modern Bibles, they contain the same message. It is logical, then, to assume that there has been no distortion of God's timeless message.

Some non-believers question whether Moses recorded a correct account of Genesis. It is reasonable to assume that he had the same pipeline to God that enabled him to predict the ten plagues. Can anyone doubt that he was tuned in on the same supernatural wavelength for all of his other information?

As for the biblical miracles, it all depends on how great you think God could be. Wasn't it God who put ten octillion stars in space? Take our planet, for example. You could fit the earth inside our sun about one and a half million times. We have a small sun and it's just one of perhaps a hundred million other suns in our galaxy. And yet our galaxy is just a speck of stardust amid a hundred million other universes known to man. The scientist Albert Einstein claimed that known space, with its hundred million universes, is only a billionth part of theoretical space.

All this movement is whirling around out there in perfect mathematical precision. We set our clocks by it. We know exactly where each planet and comet is going to be at a given point in time. To assume this just happened without a designer is like saying that parts of a complex machine could come together by accident and start functioning on its own. Just because we do not know the purpose of the universe is no reason to disbelieve it was created by a rational and intelligent hand. When you look at the universe and our planet, it's sort of put together like a giant cake. But this cake, instead of having just five or ten ingredients, has 104 elements known as the Atomic Table.

The thoroughness of God's organization of the universe also testifies to the comprehensiveness of His plan. Scientists tell us the atom is a miniature solar system. The most complex atoms have as many as 92 electrons revolving around a nucleus of 92 protons and 146 neutrons. Despite all this precise design, atheists would have us believe it came about by chance.

But God put all these elements together so they could produce life. For this to occur, the earth had to be just the exact distance from the sun. If it were too close it would be too hot to sustain life as we know it. If it was too far away, it would be too cold. The density of the earth's crust had to be just right. If it was too hard no one could plant food-stuff on it; if it was too soft, any weight would fall through it.

The tilt of the axis had to be just right, or the polar caps would melt and the earth would be flooded. The atmosphere, including hydrogen and oxygen, had to be properly mixed or people couldn't breathe. The earth must continually whirl around the sun at the right speed to hang out in space at the right distance. All of these elements combine to form life as we know it.

Life and the universe are the effect. Science says for every effect there is a cause. Only God could be the cause. Only God could create something from nothing. It doesn't seem likely that an intelligent God went to all this trouble without a purpose. Such an organized God, who had a reason for all His creativity, wouldn't leave mankind without a message spelling out what He wanted from us. The universe is proof there is an intelligent, all-powerful Creator. In the formation of the universe man can see the intelligence and power of God. But what the universe doesn't tell him is how to know God intimately. Such a God who put all these wonders out there easily could have made sure that people got His message.

Surely if God provided a message explaining His purpose, it must be in the Bible. How many books have inspired entire civilizations to base social and legal standards on their wisdom? Atheists can speculate about how it all got started, but they have no valid grounds for disputing the Bible's opening phrase: "In the beginning God created the heaven and the earth" (Genesis 1:1). To say that an orderly universe just happened would be just as absurd as if the Bible came into existence from a printing plant explosion.

Some people have difficulty accepting the Bible because it shows God accomplishing supernatural acts. A God who created the universe should be able to perform supernaturally. Why does one actually have to see them in operation before they are believable? Isn't it enough for God to do it once, then provide an authentic record?

There are many solid indications that the Bible is that authentic record. It has certain unique characteristics. First of all, it has a single theme. You can pick up most books and by the time you reach the end, you often find that the author has contradicted himself. Although the Bible was written by more than 40 men over a 1,600-year span, it is perfectly consistent. These men were kings, judges and shepherds. Yet their theme is consistent throughout.

There are passages in the Bible that are somewhat difficult to understand, but as the heavens are above the earth, so are God's ways higher than man's comprehension. And some secret things belong to the Lord. It is still God's prerogative to keep a few things to Himself.

Another evidence of the Bible's authenticity is its historical accuracy when checked against existing records. Additionally, it provides the only sensible account of certain times when no other record was available. The Bible is intelligent and it is logical. It has been confirmed many times by archaeologists who use it as a road map to buried cities and treasures. Is it surprising, then, that archaeology is Israel's favorite hobby? Israeli military training requires the study of biblical battle and escape routes in the Jewish Bible (Tenach) for use during wartime.

Perhaps the most impressive proof that the Bible is divinely inspired is that it accurately foretells the future, not in generalities, but in specific terms. Unlike human psychics, it always is right. Take the prediction in Deuteronomy 33:19, for example, which said there would be a time when people would suck treasure from the sand. Could this refer to oil wells?

Or, consider Isaiah 40:22, which tells that the earth is round. This finding was made more than 2,000 years before Columbus discovered America. Could it be that Isaiah was a scientist as well as a prophet? Or perhaps Isaiah learned this from a scholar who had talked it over with an astronomer who was far ahead of his time. Both explanations are possible, but wouldn't it be more plausible to accept Isaiah's own explanation—that his knowledge was revealed by God?

Another example of biblical knowledge explainable only by Divine authorship is in Jeremiah 31:35, where God reveals that the moon affects ocean tides. Did Jeremiah understand the gravitational pull of the moon and the stars? Was he a sailor? If not, the only explanation for such early knowledge is the one Scripture provides. It was inspired by God. Beyond this the Bible predicts, as we shall see, the reestablishment of Israel in a single day, the defeat of the

Arabs, the blossoming of the desert as a rose, and restoration of the Hebrew language.

The Bible also does everything it claims it can do. It transforms people's lives, it gives them peace, purpose, meaning and joy, and the power to live their lives on a higher plane. Both the Old and New Testaments meet these standards of inspiration. The New Covenant itself was promised in Jeremiah 31:34. God said He would give the people a new covenant, and He would write His law in their hearts and lives, and they would become His people and He their God.

The Old Covenant prophesies the coming of the Messiah; the New Covenant shows its fulfillment. Since the central belief of Messianic Judaism is that the Bible tells of a Messiah and that Yeshua is He, let's examine His credentials.

III
THE EXPECTED MESSIAH

Mainstream Judaism has always accepted the authenticity of the Tenach (Old Testament) until modern times. The New Covenant satisfies every criterion for evaluating the truth of the Old Testament. However, the authenticity of the New Covenant also depends upon the validity of the claim that the carpenter from Galilee was, in fact, the expected Messiah. Surely God must have given mankind some way of identifying the Messiah. He did indeed; fulfilled prophecy is that means. Certainly no other person has fulfilled so many prophecies so completely.

In order to fully understand why so many Jewish people did not recognize Yeshua as the Messiah, the context of the times must be seen. The Roman occupation of Israel was viewed by the populace as an intrusion upon their right to govern themselves. Although Rome permitted some local autonomy, the Jewish people longed for a leader who would extricate them from their political difficulties. It was natural for the Israelites to expect a Moses who could stand up to their oppressors, or a military revolutionary who would throw back the Roman armies. This was the hope and expectation of the people.

Fortunately for mankind, God did not provide this type of Messiah. Only one generation would have benefited.

For example, what meaning would such a political or military Messiah have for us today? Could a victory over the Romans help deal with our problems of this age? No, the Messiah was to be a moral leader; He would be of value to all generations. What the Jewish people could not see was that God had a plan for all peoples and all generations. This has been an issue among men for almost 20 centuries. Let's look at the qualifications for messiah-ship. A candidate would have to satisfy certain genealogical requirements spelled out in the Old Testament. This Messiah would have to be a son of Abraham. Genesis 22:18 says, "and in thy seed shall the nations of the earth be blessed; because thou hast obeyed my voice." But Abraham had two sons, Ishmael and Isaac. The blessing was to come through Isaac.

> "And God said unto Abraham. Let it not be grievous in thy sight because of the lad, and because of thy bondswoman; in all that Sarah hath said unto thee, harken unto her voice; for in Isaac shall thy seed be called" (Genesis 21:12).

Isaac had two sons. The Bible says the blessing would continue through Jacob.

> "I shall see Him, but not now; I shall behold Him, but not nigh; there shall come a Star out of Jacob, and a Sceptre shall rise out of Israel ... Out of Jacob shall come He that shall have dominion" (Numbers 24: 17, 19).

Jacob had twelve sons, so another choice had to be made by the Almighty. Of the twelve tribes, Judah was to be the line of promise.

> "The sceptre shall not depart from Judah, nor a lawgiver

from between his feet, until Shiloh come; and unto Him shall the gathering of the people be" (Genesis 49:10).

Out of the thousands of families in the tribe of Judah, another choice had to be made. The Messiah must come from one family line, from the family of Jesse, father of David.

"There shall come forth a rod out of the stem of Jesse, and a branch shall grow out of his roots; and the Spirit of the Lord shall rest upon him. . ." (Isaiah 11:1-2).

According to the New Covenant, the people considered Yeshua the "Son of David" and referred to Him as such. As a matter of fact, during biblical times every Jew could trace his genealogy. "So all Israel were reckoned by genealogies" (I Chronicles 9:1). These records were kept in the cities (Nehemiah 7:5,6 and Ezra 2:1). They constituted the titles to individual farms and homes. Imagine the tremendous importance given to correct genealogy. Such documents were carefully maintained until the Romans destroyed Jerusalem in 70 A.D. Thereafter, no one could claim to be the Messiah, since it could not definitely be proved they fulfilled the genealogical requirements.

There still was another, important specification about the Messiah's lineage. He must be born of a virgin.

"Therefore the Lord himself shall give you a sign, Behold the young woman (young maid or virgin) shall conceive and bear a son, and shall call his name Immanuel (God with us). Butter and honey shall he eat when he knoweth to refuse the evil and choose the good" (Isaiah 7:14-15).

The original Hebrew word for young woman is "alma."

According to today's linguistics, it can be translated as either "young maid" or "virgin". So much controversy has been attached to this prophecy and its translation, it perhaps is interesting to see how the word "alma" was translated more than a century before Yeshua's time. In the second century B.C., the Jewish scholars made about 70 translations of Scripture, which were matched in conference and resulted in what has been called the Septuagint. At that time, "alma" was translated into the Greek word "parthenos" which has only one meaning—virgin. If the interpretation merely meant a woman of young age, a number of Greek words could have been used. Furthermore, every other biblical reference to the word "alma" translates into "virgin."

When one considers the universe and its complexities, why should God's ability to create a child from a virgin be challenged? Besides, what is one unusual birth compared to God's creation of man? Man has eyes that see better than any camera. He has a brain so intricate it would take a thousand switchboards, each big enough to handle New York City, to match its complexity. It would require all the power generated by Niagara Falls to cool the computer. And it would take a structure as large as the Empire State Building to house all the equipment. Even at that, it couldn't make the decisions of an idiot if it weren't programmed by a human brain.

God created a body with many miles of blood vessels and capillaries, yet blood passes through the entire system in a matter of seconds. The entire human body goes well beyond what reasonably could happen by accident. When one ponders this and says God couldn't execute a supernatural birth, one is neither being scientific nor rational.

To further help identify the Messiah, His place of birth is given:

"But thou, Bethlehem Ephratah, though you be little

among the thousands of Judah, yet out of thee shall come forth unto that is to be ruler in Israel; whose goings forth have been from of old, from everlasting" (Micah 5:1).

Of all the continents, one was chosen—Asia; of all the States, one was selected—Canaan. All of their provinces were eliminated except Judea; only the city of Bethlehem was designated. It was a tiny village with fewer than a thousand inhabitants. Sacrificial lambs for the Passover were raised in this hamlet. The amazing birth which was to occur in Bethlehem is verified by history.

Sir William Ramsay discovered a Roman temple inscription in Turkey in 1923, which described a great tax collection ordered about four years before the birth of the Messiah. It required all Jews to travel to their ancestors' land holdings. The Jewish people, however, resented this special tax. They protested it in Rome, since the local governor didn't have authority to settle the dispute. Communication and travel was snail-paced in those days, and tax collectors were hampered by distance as well as time-consuming Jewish protests. Providence provided just enough delay to enable Miriam (Mary) to give birth to her baby in Bethlehem in fulfillment of prophecy. Bethlehem then was known as the city of David.

Its citizens eagerly anticipated the arrival of a Messiah, since the time of His coming had been foretold in Old Testament Scriptures. The prophet Daniel indicated the Messiah would come before the destruction of the Temple in 70 A.D. Daniel 9:25 says:

"Know therefore and understand that from the going forth of the commandment to restore and to build Jerusalem unto the anointed the Prince, shall be seven weeks and during three score and two weeks, the street shall be built again, with street and trench in troublous times. And after the three score and two weeks, shall the anointed be cut off and there shall be none to succeed him, and the people of the Prince that shall destroy the city and the sanctuary; and the end thereof shall be with a flood and unto the end of the war desolations are determined."

Let's study the prophecy in some detail. "Know, therefore, and understand that from the going forth of the commandment to restore and to build Jerusalem." This command was given in 445 B.C., and King Artaxerxes carried it out in the twentieth year of his reign. This is recorded in Nehemiah 2:1-8. From the commandment to restore and rebuild Jerusalem unto "the anointed the Prince" was supposed to cover a particular period of time.

The word "anointed" means Messiah. From the handing down of this commandment, the time of the Messiah would mean seven weeks and three score and two weeks. It was given in 445 B.C. From then until the Messiah's arrival would be seven weeks and three score and two weeks, or 69 weeks.

The word "weeks" in the Scriptures means "seven" in Hebrew. It also could be translated to mean that each week covers a seven-year period. It says in Genesis that Jacob worked for his uncle, Laban, for one week to obtain his wife Rachel. The context, however, indicated the Hebrew word really refers to seven years, rather than seven days. What Daniel was saying was that from the time this commandment was given until the Messiah appeared in Israel would be 69 seven-year periods, or a total of 483 years. If you move forward in time, 483 years from the command to restore and rebuild Jerusalem until the Messiah's s arrival, it brings us to 38 A.D. Taking the 483 years and subtracting the 445 from it to the year 1 B.C., leaves 38 years. There was no year zero, so by adding a year it was then 39 A.D.

Daniel's calendar was somewhat different from ours. He used the biblical calendar, which is about five days a year less than the modern calendar. When you take the five-day difference and multiply it for 483 years, it shows that Daniel had 6.6 fewer years than by today's reckoning. So when the date is adjusted it brings us to 32 A.D., when, according to Daniel 9:25-26, the anointed Prince would be cut off. Ask yourself this question: Do I know of anyone who died for the sins of the world about 32 A.D.?

If there still is any doubt about it, we've discussed the destruction of Jerusalem. Let's look at the last part of verse 26. "And the Prince that shall come shall destroy the city and the sanctuary." So the Messiah had to come and die before the Temple was destroyed.

Many of the events in the life of the Messiah also were foretold. He was to be preceded by a forerunner. Malachi 3:1—"Behold I will send my messenger, he will prepare the way before me." He also was told to be anointed with God's Spirit. Psalm 45:8—"God hath anointed thee with the oil of gladness above thy fellows." Isaiah 11:2—"And the spirit of the Lord shall rest upon him."

The Messiah also was supposed to be reproached and rejected by His Jewish brethren. He was one who was to be hated by both Romans and Jews. Psalm 69:10—". . the reproaches of them that reproached thee are fallen upon me." Psalm 69:9—"I am become a stranger unto my brethren, and an alien unto my mother's children." Psalm 69:5— "They that hate me without a cause are more than the hairs of mine head." Isaiah 49:7—"Thus saith the Lord the Redeemer of Israel and his Holy One, to him whom the nations abhor." Psalm 118:22: "The stone which the builders refused is become the head stone of the corner."

He was to be worker of miracles. Isaiah 35:5,6 says: "Then the eyes of the blind shall be opened and the ears of the deaf shall be unstopped. Then shall the lame man leap as an hart, and the tongue of the dumb sing."

He was to be beaten. Micah 4:14 says: "They shall smite the judge of Israel with a rod, upon the cheek." Isaiah 50:6 foretells, "I gave my back to the smiters, and my cheeks to them that plucked off the hair; I hid not my face from shame and spitting."

Yet the Messiah was to be meek and without violence. Isaiah 53:9 tells of His nature. "Although He had done no violence, neither was any deceit in his mouth." Similarly, Isaiah 42 prophesies: "He shall not cry nor lift up, nor cause His voice to be heard in the street."

Psalm 22, written about 1000 B.C. tells what the Messiah would say while undergoing crucifixion.

> "My God, My God, why hast thou forsaken me? All they that see me laugh me to scorn... I am poured out like water, and all my bones are out of joint; my heart is like wax; it is melted in the midst of my bowels. My strength is dried up like a potsherd; and my tongue cleaveth to my jaws; and thou hast brought me into the dust of death ... Like a lion they threaten (also translated 'they pierced') my hands and my feet... They part my garments among them, and cast lots upon my vesture. . ."

Normally death by crucifixion takes several days. So the shank bone of the victim is broken to end his misery. Yeshua died after suffering about six hours. To verify whether He was dead, a Roman soldier threw a spear into His side. When it was determined He already had expired there was no need to break the bone. This fulfilled Exodus 12:46, which says, "neither shall ye break a bone thereof," and also Psalm 34:21: "He keepeth all His bones: not one of them is broken." Oddly enough, death by crucifixion wasn't to come into being until hundreds of years after this Psalm was written.

There also are a number of other specific prophecies given hundreds of years before they occurred. The Scriptures tell of someone who was to be betrayed by a friend and sold for thirty pieces of silver, and this money was going to be thrown in the potter's field. Zechariah 11:12,13 says:

> "If ye think good, give me my price: So they weighed for my price thirty pieces of silver ... Cast it unto the potter; a goodly price that I was prised at of them. And I took the thirty pieces of silver and cast them to the potter in the house of the Lord."

Psalm 41:40 says:

> "Yea, mine own familiar friend, in whom I trusted, who did eat of my bread, hath lifted up his heel against me."

This, of course, was precisely what Judas Iscariot did with his ill-begotten reward.

The Messiah was to be pierced. "They shall look upon me for every one they have pierced, and they shall mourn for him as one mourneth for an only son. . ." (Zechariah 12:10).

There are hundreds of other prophecies in the Old Testament, all foretelling specific events. There is one chapter—all of Isaiah 53—which unmistakably is the most exciting revelation from God as to what the Messiah would be like. Even the portion of it shown below is quite convincing.

> "He was despised and rejected of men; a man of sorrows, and acquainted with grief; and as one from whom men hide their face He was despised, and we esteemed him not."

"Surely he hath borne griefs inflicted by us, and suffered sorrows we have caused: yet we did esteem him stricken, smitten of God, and afflicted. But he was wounded through our transgressions, bruised through our iniquities: the chastisement of our peace was upon him, and with his wounds we were healed. All we like sheep have gone astray; we have turned every one to his own way: and the Lord hath caused the iniquity of us all to fall upon him."

"He was oppressed, and he was afflicted, yet he opened not his mouth: as a lamb which is brought to the slaughter, and as a sheep before her shearers is dumb, so he opened not his mouth. He was taken away from rule and from judgment; and his life who shall recount? For he was cut off out of the land of the living; through the transgressions of my people he was stricken. And one made his grave among the wicked, and his tomb among the rich; although he had done no violence, neither was any deceit in his mouth."

Many Jewish people are so amazed after reading this chapter they confront their Rabbis with its accuracy. Usually the Rabbis argue that the chapter refers to a Messianic age, rather than to an individual.

Perhaps they should reconsider. Isaiah 53 couldn't refer to a Messianic age. The singular personal pronoun "he" is used consistently throughout this chapter. Secondly, it wouldn't make any sense to substitute "Messianic age" for "he." If "Messianic age" was substituted for "he," the fifth verse would read: ". . the Messianic age was wounded through our transgressions. The Messianic age was bruised for our iniquities. The chastisement of our peace was upon the Messianic age and with the Messianic age wounds are healed." This verse must be describing a person. It just doesn't make sense to talk of "chastisement" and "wounds" of a Messianic age.

Similarly, the pronoun "he" cannot apply to the Jewish people nor any of the prophets. The sixth verse says "the Lord has caused the iniquities of us all to fall on Him." Jews haven't atoned for the world, only the Messiah has. The seventh verse says, "as a lamb which is brought to the slaughter and a sheep before a shearer is dumb, so He opened not His mouth." Israel hasn't exactly been a silent sufferer and it hasn't been complacent.

Hanukkah, an annual Jewish festival, commemorates the rebellion of the Jewish people against the heathen King Antiochus Epiphanes in 165 B.C., and Jews certainly did riot and suffer in silence during the Six Day War in 1967. If Egyptian President Nasser were alive he could tell how "silent" Jews were.

The eighth verse of Isaiah 53 says that "He was cut off out of the land of the living," and the verse adds that "through (or for) the transgressions of my people, was He stricken." If "he" refers to the Jewish people, to who does "my people" refer? There seems to be a contradiction if you follow that line of reasoning.

The ninth verse says that "he had done no violence, neither was any deceit in His mouth." Does mankind commit violence or practice deceit? It certainly does. According to this same prophet, Isaiah, there is deceit in the mouth of the Jewish people. In Isaiah 6:5 it is said: "Woe is me! because I am undone because I am a man of unclean lips, and I dwell in the midst of people of unclean lips. . ."

The word Israel cannot be substituted for "he." Israel had not been without sin. For example, when Moses was on the mountain receiving the Ten Commandments, what were the Jewish people doing? They were building a golden calf and worshipping it. Moses came down and spoke to his brother, Aaron, who said the people became bored and didn't have anything to do, so they asked him to erect a golden calf. Israel hardly was sinless.

There were many other times when Scripture portrayed Israel as sinning. The Book of Hosea compares Israel to an adulterous wife. You can see the sinfulness of Israel almost anywhere in the Old Testament. Isaiah's prophecy cannot be referring to the Jewish people.

It has only been within the last few centuries—with the advent of reformed Judaism—that the Rabbis have tried to apply Isaiah 53 to a Messianic age utopia. The world is supposed to be getting better and better, according to them.

All through the ages, many Rabbis have accepted Isaiah 53 in the Scriptures as speaking of the Messiah. Rabbi Alcheck of the 16th century said of Isaiah 53: "Our Rabbis, with one voice, accept and affirm the opinion that the prophet is speaking of King Messiah." Moses Maimonides, who wrote the 13 articles of the Jewish faith, said: "I believe with perfect faith in the coming of the Messiah." Orthodox Jews still believe it. With all this evidence, any fair-minded person would have to admit there is more in these prophecies than mere coincidence. How, then, did the Jewish Pharisees miss Yeshua's coming? Why didn't they recognize Him? They certainly were learned in scriptural matters.

As we have seen in Isaiah 53, the true Messiah was to be rejected by men. It also is shown that He was to be the stone which the builders rejected (Psalm 118:22). If all the Jewish people of the time accepted Him, then He wouldn't have been rejected and wouldn't have met the criteria of this Psalm.

Actually, the scholarly Rabbinic community of the times did not recognize that Old Testament prophecies spoke of the Messiah coming twice. They assumed He would come once, deliver them from their political difficulties, and that would be it. It didn't occur to them that some of the prophecies referred to one coming in humility, and others suggested a Second Coming when He would appear as King of Kings and Lord of Lords. Since the scholars were expecting a political or military leader, they emphasized the latter prophecies regarding His power to defeat the enemies of Israel and set up a kingdom of peace.

> "In that day shall the Lord defend the inhabitants of Jerusalem; and he that is feeble among them at that day shall be as David; and the house of David shall be as God, as the angel of the Lord before them. And it shall come to pass in that day, that I will seek to destroy all the nations that come against Jerusalem" (Zechariah 12:8-9).

> "Then shall the Lord go forth and fight against those nations, as when he fought in the day of battle" (Zechariah 14:3).

With the 20/20 accuracy of hindsight, it can be seen that God meant the Messiah would appear on earth twice. The first appearance was to reconcile man and to provide a necessary sacrifice. This was so that man could be in right standing with God. The Second Coming, when Yeshua would appear as King of Kings, would come later. Yeshua had proved Himself worthy of exaltation, since He permitted Himself to be sacrificed even though He had done no wrong. His perfectly righteous blood was spilled on behalf of all mankind. This satisfied God's requirement shown in Leviticus 17:11, that "blood is the atonement for souls." Hence, mankind only can receive atonement through a sacrifice of righteous blood to offset the crimes against God which all mankind commits.

In this way, anyone who believes Yeshua's sacrifice was

made for them can have it count in God's ledger of sin debits and sacrifice credits. By believing in God's Word on this subject, it counts for righteousness, as in Abraham's case. "Abraham believed God and it was counted for him as righteousness" (Genesis 15:6).

Just as Abraham was restored to right standing with God (righteousness) by having faith in His Word, so it is when we believe in God's Word. In this case, His Word reports the sacrifice of the Messiah's righteous blood to reconcile man with his maker.

Isn't it wonderful? God provides the system, the explanation of how it works, and the required sacrifice. He also gives mankind the measure of faith required to accept it all. He does this even though mankind hasn't shown he deserves it.

As it has been shown, the Messiah was born of an unusual conception. A woman's flesh was impregnated by God's Spirit. That's why He was able to be completely righteous. The Ruach Ha Kocesh (Holy Spirit) within Him permitted Him to see the world through God's eyes.

In effect, the Messiah was the prototype of a new human being, the God-man. It was necessary for Yeshua to be born of human flesh so He could identify with our difficulties and pain. Through His death and residency in heaven, He was able to send this same comforting Spirit to dwell within us. Thus, we also can be impregnated by God's Spirit simply by repenting of our sins against God, declaring our belief in the Messiah, and asking that God's Spirit come to reside in our hearts. This is the requirement for direct access to the God of the universe, the Bible says. There never has been a case when this was done in sincerity that it didn't work. Here is a sample prayer for those who have not become personally acquainted with the God of Abraham, Isaac and Jacob.

"Dear God, I confess that I have greatly sinned against you and I'm truly sorry for it. Messiah, please come into my heart and life and cleanse me with your blood of atonement. Thank you for doing this according to your Word. I'll do anything you want me to ... with your help. I really mean it, Lord. In thy name, Amen."

By genuinely offering such a prayer, God will make Himself more and more apparent. He said He would come into us if He were asked to. "Whosoever shall call on the name of the Lord shall be delivered" (saved) (Joel 3:5). Here God made a definite promise.

Since you now have been impregnated by God's Spirit, you, too, are a God-man (or woman) who will, over time, become more and more conformed to God's image. Of course, this is not in the same sense as was the Messiah. He led a perfect life. We cannot be as righteous as He was. In God's sight, however, we share His righteousness if we accept His sacrifice by faith. After reading the New Covenant, the Old Covenant will become understandable as never before. The New Testament provides us with an overview of the God system. Try it, you'll like it.

Today, as it was 2,000 years ago, only those who are proud and haughty are unwilling to bend to God and therefore cannot see the Truth. It takes a repentant person who has needs to see God. The self-satisfied, who want God only on their terms, never will have a personal relationship with Him. The issues are the same today as they were more than 19 centuries ago.

No other man could have possibly fulfilled so many prophecies. True, post-biblical history is full of great Jewish leaders. Remember Rabbi Akiba, who hailed Bar-Cochba as the promised "Star of Jacob" and died a martyr's death? There also was Moses Mendelson, sometimes referred to as the father of modern Judaism. Karl Marx, the socialist, and

Theodore Herzl, father of Zionism, were prominent in Jewish history, as well as others too numerous to name. Yet which of them could rightly claim to satisfy the long-deferred hope of the Jewish people for a Deliverer? Which of these men rekindled the long-dormant yearning for God? None.

Political philosophies won't provide solutions. God has told us that the answers come from belief in Him. Yeshua is He of whom the prophets spoke; He is of whom Moses wrote. He is the Lamb of God. He took the penalty due mankind. He is the Prince of Peace; He is the longed for Messiah.

Although the coming of the Messiah perfectly matched biblical prophecies, His coming was not consistent with the preconceived ideas and wishful thinking of a military or political leader. What's more, Yeshua's criticism of the Pharisaic Temple leaders set off a schism which still exists. In order to clear this misunderstanding of almost 2,000 years, it is necessary to examine what occurred in the centuries immediately following the fulfillment of the prophecies cited above. Unraveling long-standing prejudices and misperceptions requires delving into their origins.

IV
EARLY MESSIANIC JEWISH HISTORY

The beginning of the conflict between the Messianic Jewish community and the Pharisaic Temple community came with the rise of Rabbinical Judaism and the increased influence of the rabbinical commentary (Mishna). Rabbinic opinion often superseded the Old Testament itself in authority. For example, one section of the Mishna states that breaking the Mosaic Law should not be punishable, but violating the law of the sages is.

Clashing doctrines of the Messiah and the Pharisees became the main source of conflict. The Pharisees were concerned with whether Yeshua would support Pharisaic Judaism and the Mishna commentaries. The New Covenant tells of conflicts centering on such things as the various traditions and the keeping of the Sabbath. The final outcome was the Sermon on the Mount where, Yeshua said, unless an individual's righteousness went beyond that of the temple leaders, he could not enter the Kingdom of God. In effect, this amounted to a rejection of Pharisaic Judaism. The Messiah's opposition to Pharisaism led to their rejection of Him and, ultimately, to His crucifixion.

Between about 30 to 66 A.D. in Messianic Jewish history, New Covenant theology was being developed. One key tenet of the New Covenant was that ritual law no longer was of critical importance since the Messiah fulfilled it. Accordingly, mankind need no longer suffer the curse of spiritual death brought on by Adam's fall. This doctrine asserted that believers could enjoy a vicarious righteousness by having faith in Yeshua. From that time on, believers could observe the ritual law if they wanted to, but it was no longer required.

Some Jews wanted to compromise. They were known as Judaizers—Jewish believers in Yeshua, but who insisted on keeping the rituals as a requirement for salvation. These men were intent on counteracting what Paul was teaching that God's salvation could only be obtained through acceptance of the Messiah.

Although mainstream Messianic Judaism agreed that the ritual law was no longer mandatory, many of them continued to practice it on a voluntary basis. The Judaizing element, however, tried to make the law obligatory. The scene changed somewhat between 66 and 70 A.D. This was during the first Jewish revolt against Rome. As the conflict intensified, Messianic Jews left the country and moved to Trans-Jordan. This created an even greater breach between the Jewish believers and the non-believing Jewish community. The Temple was destroyed in 70 A.D.

After the revolt, the Messianic Jewish community returned to the country and re-established its assembly in Jerusalem. Discussions among believers were held between 70 and 132 A.D. The Rabbis of that era called Jewish believers heretics.

Because Messianic Jews used the destruction of the Temple as proof that the Messiah had made the final sacrifice, there was an upsurge in the movement, with many Jews beginning to join it. Finally, the Rabbis decided to end these discussions and forbade any contact with the Messianic Jewish community. Messianic Jews were expelled from the synagogue. It wasn't until later that they were expelled from the community.

The Bar-Cochba Revolt occurred between 132 and 135 A.D. It was the second Jewish uprising against Roman rule. It eventually changed the nature of the dispute between Jewish believers and the Rabbinical Jewish community. Then, there was a radical change. So many non-Jews accepted Messianic claims, the movement became more and more of a Gentile religion. This marked the rejection of the Messianic movement as a force in the Jewish community.

During the first year of the revolt, Messianic Jews fought alongside their other Jewish brethren. But a year later, Rabbi Akiba declared Bar-Cochba to be the Jewish Messiah. As the result, Jewish believers pulled out of the revolt. They could not accept that concept, and it created the final split between the two Jewish communities.

It is interesting to note the irony and inconsistency of the rabbinical position. It often is asserted that a Jew ceases to be a Jew when he believes in Yeshua as the Messiah. Extending this reasoning, Rabbi Akiba wasn't Jewish anymore either, because he accepted Bar-Cochba as the Messiah. Yet he was one of the most famous Rabbis in Talmudic Judaism.

Eventually the Bar-Cochba Revolt was crushed and the Jewish community began to take its vengeance on the Messianic Jewish community. There were three major results of the revolt. First, the congregation in Jerusalem became Gentile, rather than Jewish. When the Bar-Cochba Revolt ended, Emperor Hagean rebuilt Jerusalem and placed it off limits to Jews. As far as the Romans were concerned, Messianic Jews still were Jews and hence Jerusalem was declared off-limits to them, too. Thus, the Gentiles began to move into that city. From that point on, non-Jewish believers prevailed in Jerusalem. By 135 A.D., the Jerusalem Church became a Gentile movement.

The takeover of the movement by Gentiles fit perfectly with the desire of traditional Jewish leaders to erect negative sanctions against Messianic Jews.

Secondly, the Rabbis ordered that there was to be no contact with Jewish believers. There was to be no business transactions with them. The children of Jewish believers were declared illegitimate; their sons were not to be taught a trade. No medical treatment was to be accepted from the believers. They were to be regarded as renegades and traitors. They were not to be helped when they were in need. Their food products were considered unfit for consumption; their books, sorcery. These are some examples of the ostracism experienced by Jewish believers.

According to the Midrash rabbinical commentary, anyone who was circumcised would not go to hell. But what would happen to Jewish believers, since they also were circumcised? An angel would come from heaven, the commentary claimed, to reset the foreskin so the Jewish believers could go to hell where they belonged. According to the Mishna, the testimony of a Messianic Jew should not be accepted. And Rabbi Akiba said that those who even read from the New Covenant were disqualified from the kingdom to come.

There was a third result of the Bar-Cochba Revolt. From 135 A.D. to roughly 200 A.D., Jewish believers faced a crushing dilemma. When Jewish believers were expelled from the traditional Jewish community, they had to face going it alone or try to gain acceptance in the non-Jewish community. Some shed their belief and returned to the more traditional Jewish life. Believing Jews became known as the Nazarenes. They decided to maintain their testimony of their faith in the Messiahship of Yeshua. They would go it alone and suffer expulsion.

The Nazarenes accepted the doctrines of Paul, which said that the ritual law had been rendered inoperative.

They did, however, recognize the national and cultural significance of Judaistic practices. Even when many Gentiles accepted the Messiah, Nazarenes kept their Jewish distinctiveness. Their theology was the same as Gentile Christianity. Distinction was not based on theology; it was based on nationality. Then, as now, Jews wanted to be Jews. Although they kept portions of the Mosiac Law, the Nazarenes did not require Gentiles to do likewise. So this separate existence was maintained because of loyalty to their own people, as well as nationality, despite expulsion from the Jewish community. The Nazarenes' outlook was much the same as today's Messianic Jews.

There was another group known as Ebionites, who were considered by non-Jewish believers to be heretical. They tried to combine faith in the Messiah with certain religious elements of Judaism which could not possibly be reconciled. In order to combine them, the Ebionites had to deny the virgin birth. They also had to deny the divine nature of the Messiah. Ebionites believes Yeshua was just a man who lived a perfect life and was able to fulfill the Law perfectly. By this means He became the Jewish Messiah.

Ebionites accepted only the Gospel of Matthew. They completely rejected Paul because of the Pauline doctrine of freedom from the law and its obligations. Instead, they emphasized the keeping of the Law and the necessity of circumcision. They set up their own congregations to celebrate their own rites, exalted James over Paul, and developed a somewhat distorted theology.

Meanwhile, the Gentiles were observing these difficulties within the Jewish community. Writers like Heggissipus described the Nazarenes as believing Jews. Christians considered the Nazarenes to be faithful and distinct only because they followed certain Jewish national customs.

One of the early non-Jewish writers, Justin, described this conflict as it existed in the second century. The difficulty, he pointed out, centered on two main questions: the person of the Messiah and the attitude toward the Mosaic Law. Justin's view represented the moderate Gentile Christian outlook toward Jewish believers of that period. He agreed that Jewish believers should participate in certain Jewish customs. The only thing Justin objected to was Messianic Jews making these customs mandatory. He resented extremism. He objected to the Ebionites, but he accepted the Nazarenes. And Justin divided the entire body of Messianic Jews into four distinct groups:

1—Jewish believers who were members of Gentile churches.

2—Secret Jewish believers who were members of synagogues.

3—Ebionites, who followed Jewish customs and believed it was mandatory for Gentiles to agree.

4—Nazarenes, who also kept Jewish customs, but did not consider it mandatory.

Although Jerusalem was off-limits to Messianic Jews, they were quite populous all over the rest of Israel. There were at least two villages composed entirely of Jewish believers, and many cities had large numbers of them. It is obvious from many written sources there were considerable numbers of Jewish believers throughout Israel in the second century.

Then, as now, it was difficult for a Messanic Jew to retreat. Traditional Jews considered all believers Gentiles. On the other hand, Gentiles were uneasy with them as Jews.

Meanwhile, with Gentile Christianity becoming established in its own right, the struggle began between Gentile and Jewish believers. The dispute essentially was over whether Jewish believers should be allowed to continue certain Jewish practices. A key conflict developed over the question of Resurrection Day and when it should be celebrated. It was not called Easter then. Gentile Christianity began to push for a strictly Sunday celebration; Messianic Jews disagreed.

In 196 A.D., a council was held in Caesarea, but no Jewish representatives attended. This council decreed that Resurrection Day was to be celebrated on Sunday. Messianic Jews did not object to Sunday worship since they were worshipping on Sundays anyway. They went to the synagogue on Saturday and they worshipped among themselves on Sunday. The issue was whether the resurrection of the Messiah was to be celebrated on what we now call Easter Sunday, or after the 14th day of the month of Nisan which was the date of the Passover according to the Bible.

When Messianic Jews learned of the decision, they bolted. They considered Resurrection Day impossible to change because it was fixed by the Lord Himself. In fact, Jewish believers considered Passover to be even more important than the observance of the Sabbath.

In the third century, Gentile and Jewish believers began to split over the observance of Passover. The gulf widened as the Messianic Jewish community continued to adhere to features of the Mosaic Code such as circumcision and dietary laws, as two examples.

As the Gentiles gained dominance over the movement and the Jewish believers' position became less threatening, rabbinical restrictions softened. The traditional Jewish community still was admonished not to speak to or acknowledge believers in any way. But in the second half of the century this attitude softened somewhat. The rabbinical writings of these times indicated the presence of Messianic Jewish doctors. Jewish people once again were permitted to consult with them. The Nazarenes were still considered apostate, but communication and interrelationships were permitted.

Meanwhile, the Gentile Christians were penetrating into Judea from the coast. Ever since the Greek invasion about 300 B.C., the entire coastal plain of Israel primarily had been Gentile. Most of the Gentile churches in the land were along the coastal strip.

The fourth century marked the end of the Messianic Jewish movement as such. Gentile Christian writers of this period included Apathames, Heggissipus and Jerome, all of whom were heavily influenced by Jewish believers. Among the Gentile leaders, there was a desire to consult with educated Jewish believers to discuss the theological issues. Jewish believers by this time, however, were less well-equipped theologically. They were considered less of a threat because of their diminished ability to defend their beliefs. A century earlier, when they had knowledge of the text, they were able to convince many people to believe in Yeshua.

But in the fourth century this did not occur as frequently as before. After that time the Messianic Jewish community practically stopped trying to evangelize other Jewish people. The believing Jewish community began to dwindle in numbers. In Gentile Christian writings, reference was made to Jews as "them." During the fourth century, St. Apathames even refused to acknowledge Jewish believers were Christians. He called them heretical because they celebrated Jewish festivals.

Obviously Messianic Judaism was flourishing within some form of Jewish context where these festivals were celebrated. It is difficult to visualize this occurring in a Gentile environment. As far as Gentile Christians were concerned, they were the new Israel. They thought the blessings were now going to be fulfilled in a spiritual way through the church. They considered the Nazarenes stupid for believing that biblical prophecies were to be literally fulfilled in the Jewish nation. How convenient to accept the blessings of Israel, but to leave the cursings to the Jews!

The concerns of the Jewish believers were virtually unknown to a large part of the Gentile church. They were only known among the Gentile churches in the area that was by then called Palestine. In 325 A.D., the Council of Nicea re-emphasized the importance of keeping Easter on a Sunday. None of the bishops involved in the decision were Jewish. Several years later in the Council of Antioch, they went even further. It was determined that anyone who celebrated the 14th day of Nisan as the Passover was to be excommunicated. One of the church fathers criticized Jewish believers who observed the Sabbath and practiced circumcision. This was to be the early manifestation of anti-Semitism in Gentile Christianity by well-meaning but misguided churchmen.

From the end of the fourth century onward, Messianic Judaism disappeared as a movement. From that point on, the history of the movement is a tableau of individual Jewish believers. The Messianic movement disappeared because of its inability to defend itself against majority forces—Rabbinical Judaism on the one hand; Gentile Christianity on the other.

V
THE TIMES OF THE GENTILES

The Scriptures foretold that Jerusalem would be conquered and its citizens led away in captivity. They would endure it through a period referred to as the times of the Gentiles—a time when governmental power over Israel was entrusted by God to the Gentile nations. Nation after nation has occupied Israel.

It also was a time when God brought His Holy Word to the Gentiles. The wisdom of His Word was a blessing primarily to the peoples of the world who were willing to accept Him on His terms. During this period there was a partial blindness on the Jewish people.

There is a pattern throughout the Bible that emerges with crystal clarity. From the Garden of Eden to the present time, man's spiritual state has determined his physical presence in the land of promise and plenty. Whenever the Jewish people turned from their crimes against God and earnestly sought Him, they would be restored to their land. Conversely, whenever the children of Israel turned from God, He would turn His face from them and they would lose dominion over their own land. This generation has seen Jewish people less inclined toward Rabbinism than previous ones. It also has seen Jews occupy their own land.

The Bible also tells when the times of the Gentiles would end. This was to occur when Jerusalem was no longer in Gentile hands. The Gentile age ended in 1967, when Jerusalem was back under Jewish control. This signaled the ushering in of a new era, when God would once again start to move spiritually and physically among His Jewish people. Since that time something new has been afoot.

Some 1,900 years ago, the Jewish people had a direct and personal encounter with the God of their forefathers. Many Jews realized that in the Messiah they had seen a much clearer picture of the God of Abraham, Isaac and Jacob. Most of the Jewish leaders rejected the concept of a personal relationship with God. Instead, they worshiped the god of rabbinical philosophy, national pride and social acceptance.

The Scriptures explain what has occurred spiritually to Jews, and how a spiritual blindness has happened to Israel (Isaiah 29:10). This was to continue for a limited period (Luke 21:24)—until the time Gentile domination had peaked (Romans 11:25). After then, God would once again work with the Jewish people (Isaiah 59:20, Jeremiah 31:31-34). This already has begun.

There is a strong evidence suggesting that more Jews have accepted the Messiah of the Old and New Testaments since the Six Day War then in all the previous 1,900 years combined. Moreover, most of these completed Jews see no inconsistency between their acceptance of a personal Messiah and their remaining Jewish.

They understand why God took the form of a man. To teach the law of natural physics to a colony of ants, one probably would want to become an ant. So it was that God sent a part of Himself to give us understanding.

As a man, He experienced human emotions, physical pain and anguish just as other men do. He was human in every sense. He had to be in order to correct the mess another man—Adam—got humanity into.

Even though He had done nothing wrong, He would permit His righteous blood to be spilled as a sacrifice to offset transgressions against God. He had the nature of a lamb and would be sacrificed. This would establish an infinite amount of credit to balance the scales in heaven and pay for the sins of mankind.

Only God could manifest such love. Who but God could love people so much that He would send His son to lay down His life, even for those who tormented Him? What an act of love for humanity! He did this even though mankind wasn't worthy of it. All that God asked in return was faith that He had accomplished all that was necessary for our salvation. In this way it is indeed possible for believers to get something for nothing. What a little nothing man gives for such a treasure! Unfortunately, many Jewish people were so taken with pride in being the chosen people they forgot what they were chosen to be-a holy people.

God indeed was offended. As in the past, Jewish people were to suffer double for their iniquity. After the destruction of the Temple, the Romans dispersed the Jews in large numbers from their homeland. In time, Jews were even refused access to Jerusalem.

In the third, fourth and fifth centuries, Christianity had grown from a sect of Judaism to an independent religion spread throughout many nations. These Gentile nations were still worshipping idols. Although many thousands of Jews followed after their Messiah, there were millions of Gentiles who accepted Him as their Saviour.

The cultural forms of Judaism naturally were alien to the peoples of these many lands, but the true Gentile believers had come into biblical Judaism by faith. They had become part of a great heritage of faith because they believed in a Jewish Messiah. Such Gentiles were, in effect, a new branch grafted into an old tree. As politics would have it, however, the cultural imprint of the Gentiles was to be dominant since there were so many of them and so few Jewish believers in the Messiah.

Conveniently, the church assumed that God was through with Jews. Its leaders reasoned that Jews had their chance and rejected God. It was as though the second born did not want the wayward first-born prodigal son to return.

Satan, God's adversary, cultivated this line of thought. Here we see the seeds of anti-Semitism within the institutional church. God is not anti-Semitic. He only permitted Satan to distort Christianity because it would be easier for the nations to accept salvation if they did not have to accept Jewish culture.

The sins of the Jewish people separated them from God. His people were to suffer for these transgressions because God chastens those He loves (Proverbs 3:11,12). He loved Israel since it was the "apple of His eye." The many centuries of chastening were to bring such sorrow to His stubborn people which will continue until Israelites turn from their way to God's way.

During the fifth and sixth centuries, many restrictions were placed on Jews throughout Europe. They were forbidden public office and many thousands were slain.

In 622 A.D., Mohammed naturally expected many Jewish followers. After all, he had incorporated the Torah (five books of Moses) and had relegated Yeshua to the station of prophet. Jews, however, weren't buying this decision. Mohammed then proceeded to kill most of the Arabian Jews, and the blood bath continued as his armies swept through Eastern Europe, Spain and North Africa. The so-called Christian armies stopped the Arab menace in 732 A.D. Then they concentrated on punishing Jews, driving them from the land.

During the 11th century, great crusades attempted to drive the Moslems from the Holy Land. As they marched they sang, "Why go to the land of Palestine to kill the enemies of God. Kill a Jew and save your soul." Hundreds of thousands of Jews were slain and it didn't save one soul.

One must remember that most of the world's peoples were illiterate, uninformed and understood little about true Christianity. All they knew was what the institutional church wanted them to know. They had little chance for a personal relationship with God. Since Jews never have distinguished between those who merely call themselves Christians and those who have come to be real Christians by truly knowing God, Jews never have had much respect for Christianity.

In 1298 A.D., a new wave of persecution in Europe killed hundreds of thousands of Jews. The Black Plague killed about one-fourth of Europe's population in 1350. Naturally Jews were blamed and accused of poisoning the water in response to the persecution they suffered. The fact that Jews were dying of this plague, too, apparently went unnoticed.

The Roman Catholic Church began its inquisition in 1411. Tens of thousands were put to the rack; many thousands died. Jews scarcely were regarded as human beings.

Later, the Russian Czars mistreated some five million Jews. Tens of thousands were killed and hundreds of thousands fled. In 1881, Alexander III, head of the Russian church, made it public policy that one-third of the Jews there were to die, a third were to be emigrated, and the remainder were to join the church by force, if necessary. Other governments tried to intercede, but the Russian church replied: "Jews have brought their troubles on themselves."

In our own time we all know of the Nazi massacre of six million Jews.. Yet through all this suffering, God preserved His Jewish people so that the Scriptures' promises would not be broken.

If God had wanted Jews assimilated, there certainly had been ample opportunity. It is apparent He was preserving them supernaturally in order to fulfill His eternal covenant with their ancestors. Reflect for a moment. If every Jew in the world had become assimilated into Gentile churches, they no longer would be a distinguishable people. Who then would inherit Israel?

Isn't it obvious? God's plan is to preserve the Jewish people. Who, then, has been trying to obliterate the Jews but the devil himself? If all Jews became part of the Christian church and assimilated, Satan would have accomplished what he could not do through centuries of bloodshed.

The Gentile believer in Messiah should ask himself which side he wishes to cooperate with—God or Satan. If the answer is God, Messianic Gentiles should stop trying to get Jews to abandon their Jewish heritage in order to accept the Messiah. It isn't much that Jews have to accept Christianity: so-called Christians have to accept the Jewish Messiah.

For nearly 2,000 years, the institutionalized church has been trying to get a message across to Jewish people. It has been unsuccessful largely because it tried to get Jews to give up their identity.

It is the Gentile who is not following the Messiah if he denies his Jewish roots. The New Testament cannot stand without the supporting structure of the Old Testament. No plant can survive without nurturing itself on the soil in which it is embedded.

The Messiah never forgot He was a Jew. If a Gentile really wants to be like his Messiah, he should become more interested in biblical Judaism. Nowhere in the Bible does it say a Jew becomes a Gentile when he believes the Scriptures. This is the key; it is what has been lacking over the centuries. Once this false idea has been put to rest in both the Jewish and Gentile communities, then Jews will look at the New Covenant with open eyes. Then God will have mercy on His ancient people.

Every person born of the Spirit of God should be thrilled to see the time when God once again is moving among Jewish people. This phenomenon was promised by God for the very last days. In a way, Jewish acceptance of their Messiah is a barometer of how little time mankind has left before God passes final judgment upon the world.

There will come a time when Jews everywhere will believe in Yeshua. According to the prophet Zechariah, they shall look upon Him whom they have pierced and there shall be great mourning. Then all shall know Him. Jeremiah put it best: "They shall all know Jehovah from the least of them even to the greatest of them" (Jer. 31:34).

God is giving the Jewish people a last chance to declare their allegiance before judgment comes upon the earth. Finally, after thousands of years, Jewish people are easing away from Rabbinism and looking for something more than lighting candles and observing man-made laws. Many are becoming atheists, agnostics, occultists and the like— wandering from one extreme to another—but at least they are now more open-minded. As they turn from their religion fashioned by man, God is showing His mercy. He is removing the veil from their minds so they can have eyes that see and ears that hear.

These Jewish believers cherish their heritage and subscribe to its biblical tenets, not because they have to, but out of love for their God.

VI
THE FIG TREE TAKES ROOT

The New Covenant refers to the time when Yeshua told the disciples about future cataclysmic events. They asked Him when these events would occur. Yeshua advised them to learn the parable of the fig tree. He said when its branches blossomed, summer was close at hand. Yeshua was saying, in effect, note the signs of the times. Similarly, when the symbolic fig tree (Israel) would come to life, unusual events would begin to transpire. The hearts of fearful men would fail, distress and perplexity would engulf nations, and the Second Coming of the Messiah, with all His great power and glory, would take place.

Israel is referred to as "the fig tree" many times in the Bible. God said, "I found Israel like grapes in the wilderness, I saw your fathers as the first-ripe in the fig tree" (Hosea 9:10). Joel 1:7 refers to Israel when he speaks of "barking my fig tree."

Indeed, the fig tree—Israel—is in bloom today. This ancient land and its people are coming to life in wondrous ways. This was accurately foretold thousands of years ago. The blossoming of the fig tree—Israel's development—is concrete evidence that the Bible was written by a Providential God who does not make mistakes. He knows the end from the beginning. Prophets and kings have longed to see this generation come. And now, more prophecies are being fulfilled in this generation than in any other since the first century.

Believers do not serve a capricious God. He plainly spelled out His ground rules. He said to Israel, be good and receive blessings. And he warned not to be bad for cursings surely would come. He said obedience would result in the Jewish people securing their land, and disobedience would result in their scattering. Further, a return to obedience would result in a gathering from all the nations to which Jews have been scattered.

> "And it shall come to pass, if thou shalt hearken diligently unto the voice of the Lord thy God, to observe and do all his commandments which I command thee this day, that the Lord thy God will set thee on high above all nations of the earth" (Deuteronomy 28:1).

Thus, the Lord promised blessings for obedience. But an all-knowing God realized that the weakness of man's intrinsic nature would not always permit him to obey. He warned what would happen if Israel did not heed His Word.

> "But it shall come to pass, if thou will not hearken unto the voice of the Lord thy God, to observe, to do all His commandments and His statutes which command thee this day; that all these curses shall come upon thee and overtake thee" (Deuteronomy 28:15).

One of the most far-reaching consequences, of disobedience was the scattering of Israel throughout the nations. This promise came true some 1,500 years after it was told to Moses. This prediction accurately described the precarious fate of the Hebrews Jews have been in dispersion because they disobeyed God. This dispersion was to have lasted almost 2,000 years.

> "And among these nations shalt thou find no ease, neither shall the sole of thy feet have rest; but the Lord shall give thee there a trembling heart and failing eyes and sorrow of the mind; and thy life shall hang in doubt before thee; and thou shalt fear night and day, and shall have no assurance of life: In the morning thou shalt say, 'Would God it were even!' and at even thou shalt say, 'Would God it were morning!'. . ye shall be sold unto your enemies for bondsmen and bondswomen, and no man shall buy you" (Deuteronomy 28:65-68).

Here is a picture of a really down-and-out people. Jews were treated as the dregs of the earth. God, however, had made an unconditional promise to Abraham and to his seed. He tells of the initial blessings and subsequent cursings. He also foretells Jews returning to the faith of their ancestors. He also promises a regathering.

> "And it shall come to pass when all things are come upon thee, the blessings and the curse, which I have set before thee, and thou shalt call them to mind among all the nations ... and shalt obey His voice ... then the Lord thy God will turn thy captivity, and have compassion upon thee, and will return and gather thee from all the nations, whither the Lord thy God hath scattered thee... and the Lord thy God will bring thee into the land which thy fathers possessed, and thou shalt possess it; and he will do thee good, and multiply thee above thy fathers" (Deuteronomy 30:1-5).

Oh, how God wanted Israel to be blessed and not

cursed! He pleaded with Israel. Beyond promises based on the moral conduct of Israel, the prophets also foretell of God acting on behalf of Israel, without any mention of their deserving favorable treatment.

> "And it shall come to pass in that day that the Lord shall set His hand again the second time to recover the remnant of His people... And He shall set up an ensign for the nations, and shall assemble the outcasts of Israel and gather together the dispersed of Judah from the four corners of the earth" (Isaiah 11:11,12).

In a way, God had to first put Israel in a hopeless position. Then it could see how difficult it was for their human nature to do good. Man would learn he could not be righteous through his own initiative. Instead, he could only resolve his difficulties through God's unmerited favor (grace).

> "For the Lord will have mercy on Jacob, and will yet choose Israel, and set them in their own land; and the strangers shall be joined with them, and they shall cleave to the house of Jacob ... and they shall take them captives, whose captives they were; and they shall rule over their oppressors. And it shall come to pass in the day that the Lord shall give thee rest from their sorrow, and from thy fear, and from the hard bondage wherein thou wast made to serve" (Isaiah 14:1-3).

Scripture is quite specific about the magnitude of the project to reassemble God's children from the four corners of the earth. The beginnings of this already has taken place in our lifetime. God says He will say to the north, "give up." How much one is reminded of the now familiar expression, "free Soviet Jewry." It is interesting to note that Moscow is almost due north of Jerusalem.

"Fear not for I am with thee; I will I bring thy seed from the east and gather thee from the west; I will say to the north, give up; and to the south, keep not back; bring my sons from far, and my daughters from the ends of the earth. . ." (Isaiah 43:5-7).

The prophet Jeremiah makes reference to this regathering in several biblical passages. He tells of God's mercy and of the historical importance associated with it. Jeremiah predicted that it would be an even greater miracle than the deliverance of Jews from Egyptian bondage. For 3,500 years the Jewish people have referred to God as "He who delivered us from Egypt." God says His ancient people will refer to Him as "He who regathered us."

"Therefore, behold the days come saith the Lord, that it shall no more be said, The Lord liveth, that brought up the children of Israel out of the land of Egypt; but the Lord liveth that brought up the children of Israel from the land of the north, and from all the lands whither he had driven them. . ." (Jeremiah 16:14,15).

Here, God was referring to a specific group of people. He was not speaking metaphorically about all believers. He referred to a people He led out of Egypt. Only the Jewish people have celebrated this event and have referred to God in this way.

Jeremiah also tells us about bringing Soviet Jews to Israel. This was an amazing prediction. Russia needs Jewish brainpower. Jews are among the most educated in all Russia. Even though some are being ransomed, there is a day coming when vast numbers will leave Russia. Barbed wire and machine guns are no match for the God of Israel "that shall neither slumber nor sleep."

"Therefore, behold, the days come; saith the Lord
that they shall no more say, the Lord liveth which
brought up his children of Israel out of the land of
Egypt; but the Lord liveth, which brought up and
which led the seed of the house of Israel out of the
north country, and from all countries whither I have
driven them; and they shall dwell in their own land"
(Jeremiah 23:7,8).

Jeremiah also makes clear to the Jewish people that it
was God who caused their difficulties and dispersion.
Throughout the Old Testament, God only punished for
wrongdoing. Since the destruction of Jerusalem and the
subsequent dispersion that occurred shortly after the crucifixion, it could be that Jewish rejection of God caused their
punishment. What other explanation can be offered? Is God
not just? The Bible explains that He chastens those He loves.
Once the punishment was over, He promised to take this
rag-tag remnant and guide them to the waters of spiritual
life. He would keep them on a surefooted path and care for
them as a shepherd tends to his flock.

"... the blind and the lame, the woman with child,
and her that travaileth with child together... They
shall come with weeping and with supplications will
I lead them. I will cause them to walk by the rivers
of waters in a straight way, wherein they shall not
stumble... He that scattered Israel will gather him and
keep him, as a shepherd does his flock" (Jeremiah
31:7-9).

The prophet explains that God was angry with the
Hebrews, but He looks forward to when He will be their
God and they will be His people. When this occurs, Israel
will have national security no army can provide.

> "I will bring them again unto this place and I will cause them to dwell safely; and they shall be my people, and I will be their God" (Jeremiah 32:37,38).

Another prophet also told of this regathering. Ezekiel spoke of this same event, but alluded more to the land itself. He said God was going to do this with His fury poured out and when the Jewish people arrived in the land, He would feed them on the mountains and the rivers.

> "...and will bring them to their own land, feed them upon the mountains of Israel by the rivers, and in all the inhabited places of the country" (Ezekiel 34:13).

Scriptures also tell of irrigating and tilling the soil where it previously was uninhabitable. Ezekiel said the deserted cities could be repopulated and that the Jewish people would once again possess their promised land.

> "Therefore say, thus saith the Lord God: I will even gather you among the people, and assemble you out of the countries where ye have been scattered, and I will give you the land of Israel" (Ezekiel 11:17).

Ezekiel reports that the Almighty intended not only to regather His people, but that it would be a sweet prospect to God. After all, God has been waiting a long time for His first chosen to return to Him. He relishes restoring them from their dispersion.

> "I will accept you with your sweet savor, when I bring you out from the people...and I will be sanctified in you before the nations, and ye shall know that I am the Lord, when I shall bring you into the land of Israel, into the country for which I lifted up mine hand to give it to your father" (Ezekiel 20:41-42).

God has the capacity to forgive and forget transgressions. He promises to cleanse Israel of her iniquities and to resume His program for that land. This prophecy says that people will find the progress made in the land remarkable. All the world has marvelled at how this formerly desolate land has come to life.

> "Thus saith the Lord God: In the day that I shall have cleansed you from all of your iniquities I will cause the cities to be inhabited and the wastes shall be builded, And the desolate land shall be tilled, whereas it lay desolate in the sight of all that passed by. And they shall say, This land that was desolate is become like the garden of Eden; and the waste and desolate and ruined cities are become fortified, and are inhabited. Then the nations that are left round about shall know that I the Lord build the ruined places, and plant that that was desolate. . ." (Ezekiel 36:33-38).

Ezekiel also said that the Jewish people would be regathered after they have borne their shame. In other words, the shame of the Jews will end when they have been regathered. The prophet spoke of the present time. If the sentence is ending for Jews, then their partial blindness also must be lifting. If Jews have suffered enough because of their sins, then He will no longer hide Himself from them. The evidence of this is clear. More and more Jews are wearing a special smile these days.

> "... Now I will bring again the captivity of Jacob, and have mercy upon the whole house of Israel ... after that they have borne their shame, and all their trespasses whereby they have trespassed against me...When I have brought them again from the people, and gathered

them out of their enemies' lands, and am sanctified in them in the sight of many nations; then shall they know that I am the Lord their God, which caused them to be led into captivity among the heathen. . ." (Ezekiel 39:25-28).

Other prophets also told of God's strong affection and allegiance to Israel, and how He promised to stand by her and restore her strength.

It should be apparent by now that the same God which physically scattered Israel is regathering its ancient people. God was not speaking metaphorically. He was foretelling history. He wasn't speaking of a Gentile church which had not yet come into existence. He was speaking of a real people undergoing real trial. He was speaking of hardship and of the destiny of the Jewish people.

Today there are well meaning, but mistaken, theologians who would spiritualize these prophecies so they only would be an allegory referring to the Christian church. Such men, for all practical purposes, would deny these actual events occurred and still are happening to the Jewish people today. These theologians are suggesting that God is through with the Jewish people and only is concerned with the church. They are ignoring the obvious straight-forward message concerning the Jewish people and their land. This is not to say that physical events do not have spiritual parallels.

How can anyone deny that history is fulfilling the promises of the land to Abraham. In 1897, Theodore Herzl called the first Zionist Congress in Basel, Switzerland. These men dreamed of a Jewish state. By bribing Turkish officials, Jews with a similar dream were able to enter Palestine. Here was a homeland for Jews scattered all over the world. Their plan was to establish a foothold in Arab territory. Secondly, they wanted the land to be under the control of a friendly power. The third stage was to get the land in the hands of the Jewish people. This plan must have been inspired because that is exactly what happened.

During World War I, Jews were in many European battle zones. The advance of the Russian armies meant pogroms bringing terror and violence upon Jews. At this time, Great Britain was in a desperate situation with a shortage of gunpowder made of nitrates imported over waters controlled by German submarines. Chaim Weizmann, a brilliant Jewish scientist, discovered how to make gunpowder from nitrogen in the air.

To express its appreciation, the British Parliament adopted the Balfour Declaration which supported establishment of a Jewish homeland. On December 11, 1917, General Allenby took the city of Jerusalem from the Turks without firing a shot. He owed this to an ancient battle recounted in the Bible. After World War I, the League of Nations gave Great Britain a mandate to control the land of Palestine.

Hitler's extermination of Jews in Europe during World War II sent them clamoring for entrance into Israel. But Britain didn't want trouble with the Arabs and refused to let Jews enter Palestine except for a nominal number. However, the terrible slaughter of six million Jews created worldwide sympathy for the plight of survivors. This eventually resulted in creation of the State of Israel by the United Nations in 1948. The first Arab-Israeli war over the newly acquired land, and those since, have seen Israel persevere against superior numbers and equipment. God had miraculously intervened and the new nation of Israel was held together.

For centuries, no Jews were allowed in Jerusalem and only a handful were in all of Palestine. By 1882, about 24,000 Jews had managed to get into the land. But by 1947, there were 626,000. On May 14, 1948, Prime Minister David Ben Gurion proclaimed the statehood of Israel in Tel Aviv's Museum Hall. One is reminded of Isaiah 66:8:

"...shall the earth be made to bring forth in one day? Or shall a nation be born at once?"

In Israel's first seven months as a nation, 100,000 refugees arrived, and a total of 340,000 were admitted during the first 18 months. Within three years, some 655,000 had returned.

The arrival of so many people from so many countries created a great deal of confusion. Everyone spoke different languages. This prompted an Israeli editor, Eliezar Ben Yehuda, to re-establish Hebrew as the national language of Israel. The Hebrew Bible has some 7,700 words. Many new words were added to modernize the language and account for the phenomena unknown in biblical days. This was the prophetic fulfillment of the restoration of a language virtually dead since the 6th century B.C.

> ". . . As yet they shall use this speech in the land of Judah and in the cities thereof, when I shall bring again their captivity. . ." (Jeremiah 31:23).

> "For then will I turn to the people a pure language, that they may call upon the name of the Lord, to serve him with one consent" (Zephaniah 3:9).

But gathering the people, winning the war and re-establishing a dormant language was not all God was doing. Modern cities, such as Haifa and Tel Aviv, sprang up. Israel began to build the "waste cities," fulfilling the words of Amos.

> "And I will bring again the captivity of my people of Israel, and they shall build the waste cities, and inhabit them, and they shall also plant vineyards, and drink the wine thereof; they shall also make gardens and eat the fruit of them. And I will plant them upon their land,

and they shall be no more pulled up out of their land which I have given thee. said the Lord thy God" (Amos 9:14,15).

Modern Israelis tilled the desert soil with tractors, while they carried machine guns for defense. How can one help but remember the story in the fourth chapter of Nehemiah about those who built the wall of Jerusalem with one hand and held their weapons with the other.

What was once a barren and lonely place became a green field and a fertile valley. This fulfilled the prophecy which said "the wilderness and the solitary place shall be glad for them. And the desert shall rejoice and blossom as the rose" (Isaiah 35:1).

How true it is, Israel grows cold and warm weather crops together in some parts of the country. Agriculture now is one of Israel's greatest resources. The planting of millions of tree forests reminds one of Ezekiel 36:30: "I will multiply the fruit of the trees."

Israel's neighbors, though, were not content to live in peace, and Egypt's President Nasser began to summon Arab leaders for an all-out attack on Israel. He succeeded in convincing United Nations Secretary General U Thant to remove the U.N. Security Force which policed buffer zones between Israel and her antagonists. Arabs went into a frenzy as they prepared for a holy war to annihilate every last Jew. Confident that their armies, representing 82 million Arabs, could easily defeat the Israeli nation of only 2½ million Jewish people, they mobilized for all-out warfare. Israel's military leaders conferred in urgent meetings. Their religious leaders and soldiers met and prayed in Israel's hour of trial.

What occurred in the next six days made the ears of the world tingle. Israel more than doubled her land area. Complete columns of Arab armor were abandoned, not because they were destroyed by Israeli military hardware, but because of the fear in the hearts of the Arabs. Russian missiles also were abandoned, even though they were poised for firing. Their Arab operators fled in fear of their lives. And the Scriptures were fulfilled: "In that day shall Egypt be like unto woman, and the land of Judah shall be a terror unto Egypt because of the council of the Lord of hosts, which he hath determined against it" (Isaiah 19:16,17).

The battle was carried to the holy city of Jerusalem. On June 7, 1967, Defense Minister Moshe Dayan and the Israeli army entered the Jordanian sector of Jerusalem for the first time in more than 2,500 years. Jerusalem at last was under the control of the Jewish people. Chief Military Rabbi Goren offered prayers of thanksgiving in the narrow alley in front of the Wailing Wall.

Who can deny God has done miraculous things to fulfill His Word. Jews have been preserved throughout history because God has a wonderful purpose for them. If God has meant for His promises only to apply to spiritual Israel (Christians), then why is He doing all this in Israel today? Jews have not become extinct. If the Bible only was referring to the Christian church, events of the last few decades wouldn't have occurred. Just as God made His promises concerning the land come to pass, He also will make Jews as a nation turn back to the biblical faith of their forefathers. What a joy it is for Jew and Gentile alike to help prepare Israel for her national day of salvation!

VII
THESE DRY BONES LIVE

The prophet Ezekiel had an amazing vision concerning Israel. He described it this way:

> "The hand of the Lord was upon me, and carried me out in the spirit of the Lord, and set me down in the midst of the valley which was full of bones ... they were very dry. And he said unto me, Son of man, can these bones live?" (Ezekiel 37:1-5).

This was a graphic description of a valley filled with parched bones. Since they were extremely dry and brittle, it is reasonable to assume that they had been in this condition for some time. These bones also must have been far from any moisture in order to be so dry. Water is the means of life to every living thing. Without it, mankind shrivels and dies. One cannot help but remember the living waters spoken of by Yeshua in the New Covenant. He promised living waters to any who would believe in Him. These are waters that well up from within us and satisfy our spiritual thirst.

In a way, ancient Judaism cut itself off from these living waters when it rejected the Messiah. Since then, the life has slowly drained from traditional Jewish faith. In fact,

many Jewish people today are searching for more stimu-
lation in their worship services and no longer find ritual
to be meaningful to their lives.

The same could be said of much of the institutional
church. In many quarters it, too, has become dried up.

> "Thus saith the Lord God unto these bones; Behold,
> I will cause breath to enter into you, and ye shall
> live; and I will lay sinews upon you, and will bring
> up flesh upon you, and cover you with skin, and put
> breath in you ... and ye shall live. . ." (Ezekiel 37:6).

God says He can and will restore the former vitality.

> "... and as I prophesied, there was a noise, and behold
> a shaking, and the bones came together bone to bone.
> And when I beheld, lo, the sinews and the flesh came
> upon them, and the skin covered them above; but
> there was no breath in them. Then said he unto me,
> Prophesy unto the wind, prophesy, son of man, and say
> to the wind, Thus saith the Lord God; come from
> the four winds, O breath, and breathe upon these
> slain, that they may live" (Ezekiel 37:7-9).

The noise could be referring to an abrupt change that is
occurring among Jews and also in the institutional church.
God not only is putting these bones back in their proper
order; He also is binding them together with muscle and
tissue. According to this prophecy, breath will come into
these restored forms. This breath will come from the four
winds. The fulfillment of prophecy concerning Jews and
their restoration to the land is causing believers to live in
expectation of even more momentous events.

"So I prophesied and he commanded me, and breath

came into them, and they lived and stood upon their feet, an exceeding great army. Then he said unto me, Son of man, these bones are the whole house of Israel: behold, they say, Our bones are dried, and our hope is lost; we are cut off for our parts ... Behold, O my people, I will open your graves and cause you to come up out of your graves, and bring you into the land of Israel. And ye shall know that I am the Lord when I have opened your graves ... And shall put my spirit in you, and ye shall live, and I shall place you in your own land; then shall ye know that I the Lord have spoken it, and performed it, saith the Lord" (Ezekiel 37:10-14).

These bones—the house of Israel—live. God's sovereignty is opening up the tombs of a people who have suffered spiritual death. He also is putting His Spirit into them so they might become a mighty spiritual army.

God promises to take the old, dried up, disjointed bones of Israel and fashion them into a living entity. Ezekiel speaks of restored life for the Jewish people. Instead of existing in a hopeless and lost condition, cut off from their ancestral parts, God tells His intention to restore Jews to their own land.

After hundreds of years of being spiritually disjointed and dispersed, God not only is going to restore the Jewish people to their land, He also is going to restore the faith of their forefathers in them. Zechariah 3:15-20 relates that God would regather Israel to Himself, and rest in His love, just contemplating them with joy. Just as spiritual disunity from God coincided with dispersion from Israel, so it was that the regathering is occurring at a similar time as their spiritual awakening.

This is causing many in the church to re-evaluate their previous assumptions about the Jewish people. For some time it was commonly assumed that while the Old Testament had to do with earthly things, the New Covenant was concerned with heavenly matters. This view implied that the people of the Old Testament (Jews) were concerned solely with earthly matters. It therefore was thought that they could have no place in the superior realm. Similarly, this view suggested that the heavenly people (Christians) would be in the higher realm. But such a clear-cut distinction between earthly and heavenly matters is faulty.

Throughout the Bible, the occupation of the land of Canaan had meaning beyond the mere possession of territory. It enabled the people to commune more closely with God and obey His commandments. The return of Jewish people to Israel has been consistently linked to the righteousness of the people. This relationship is clearly shown in Isaiah 60:21.

> "Thy people shall be all righteous and they shall inherit the land forever, the branch of my planting, the work of my hands, that I may be glorified."

Because of their ancient romance, the Almighty never intended for Jewish people to be permanently separated from Him. God frequently referred to Israel as His sweetheart and wife. He spoke of her in Isaiah 54 as a woman forsaken and grieved in spirit, and as a young wife. He even planned to tear up the bill of divorce which He gave to her (Isaiah 50:1). In fact, God promised Israel and Judah a new covenant.

> "Behold, the days come, saith the Lord, that I will make a new covenant with the house of Israel and with the house of Judah: Not according to the covenant that I made with their fathers in the day that I took them by the hand to bring them out of the land of Egypt ... But this shall be the covenant that I will

make with the house of Israel: After those days, saith
the Lord, I will put my law in their inward parts, and
write it in their hearts; and will be their God, and
they shall be my people ... for they shall all know
me from the least of them unto the greatest of them,
saith the Lord; for I will remember their sin no more"
(Jeremiah 31:30-33).

God has made His New Covenant. The details of the
contract are spelled out in the New Testament. There simply has been a 1,900-year delay for most Jewish people
in finding out this agreement applies to them.

There also is a parallel between events of the first century and those of today. A pattern emerges from a broad
review of Jewish history. As history moved beyond the first
century the Messianic movement became less Jewish in outlook, with fewer Jews joining in it. With the 20th century
nearing its end, there is a greater awareness of Christianity's
Jewish roots. There also is more emphasis on Jewishness
by Jews who have accepted the New Covenant. As the result, we are seeing more and more Jews accepting the Messiah. It is as though the first century Messianic Judaism
is being revisited. Observers should not find this unusual.

As the Second Corning of the Messiah approaches,
the entire process appears to be working in reverse. About
200 years ago, it was unthinkable that Jews could accept
the Messiah and still be Jewish. Completed Jews were
absorbed into Gentile culture. Occasionally, a scholar
would take an unusual academic interest in his former
Jewish heritage. It has only been during the past 100 years
that the church has become aware that Christianity cannot
stand without its Jewish foundations. Today, scholars
fully realize that the New Covenant can best be understood
in the context of first century Jewish history.

It wasn't until the latter part of the 1800's that a new

phenomenon began to emerge. It was called Hebrew Christianity. For the first time in modern memory, Jewish believers in the New Covenant identified themselves as a distinct entity. At the time, the use of the term "Hebrew Christian" was quite controversial.

Some people even thought Jews were separating themselves from the church with this identity. Despite the controversy attached to it, many Jewish believers persisted in this identification because it was obvious to them that God wanted a remnant preserved. A desire to meet with like fellows resulted in formation of the Hebrew Christian Alliance of America in 1915. Similar organizations were formed in other nations, resulting in an International Hebrew Christian Alliance.

After the 1967 Arab-Israeli war, pride in Jewishness was accelerated by both traditional Jews and Jewish believers. It was only natural that new Jewish believers sought stronger identification as Jews. They no longer wanted to be known as a special kind of Christian; they wanted to be described as a type of Jew. They no longer wanted their heritage to be a footnote. Such Jews wanted their belief in the Messiah to label them as a type of Jew, a true Jew, a biblical Jew, a Jew who believes in the Messiah—a Messianic Jew.

As Jewish people understand that the New Covenant enhances, rather than replaces their Judaism, they are investigating the New Covenant in growing numbers. If you want fewer Jews to accept the Messiah, make the faith less Jewish. If you want more Jews to accept Him, reinforce the Jewishness of the faith.

In the late 1960's, America's youth was in the forefront of change. So it was among Jewish believers. The recent upsurge in Messianic Judaism largely has been spearheaded by enthusiasm of young Jewish believers. Public demonstrations, magazine articles, Jews for Jesus parades, and Messianic congregations largely are projects undertaken by people in their thirties and younger. These young people particularly were stirred by biblical prophecy concerning Israel being fulfilled.

Some church leaders say the prophecies concerning Israel are for spiritual Israel (the church). Other Jewish scholars argue that these prophecies are for the descendents of Jacob. Actually, both positions are correct and they do not contradict one another. These prophecies not only are literally coming true for the land of Israel, but also figuratively for spiritual Israel. Thus, there is a parallel between the physical fate of that small nation and the spiritual life of the body of believers in the Messiah. God works on more than one level at a time. The dry bones described by Ezekiel not only refer to the coming together of physical Israel, they also refer to the institutional church coming to a greater spiritual life.

The bones Ezekiel saw coming together also could refer to the spiritual body of believers working in greater harmony. Each bone may represent a different denomination. They all have different functions, yet they are being reunited into a great army. God is breathing life into dead institutions.

VIII
MEMBERS OF THE FAITH RACE

Messianic Judaism fosters a unity between Jews and Gentiles. In the Spirit of God there is no difference between Jew or Gentile, man or woman.

The Spirit of God recognizes no preference or superiority. This does not mean we are all the same. Equal does not mean identical. Men and women are different, but who would want it otherwise? The same is true of Jews and non-Jews.

However, simply because people are of like faith does not mean they all are the same. In the animal kingdom, birds are not superior to fish and fish are not superior to birds. In spirit and in heaven, a Jewish soul is not more valuable than a Gentile soul. In the spiritual realm, all believers are one.

After all, wasn't the first Jew Abraham, and wasn't he born a Gentile? By definition, the first Jew had to be of Gentile parentage. Faith in God's Word was what made Abraham unusual. The Scriptures say of Abraham: "And he believeth in the Lord; and He counted it to him as righteousness" (Genesis 15:6). Mankind is in the same position today as Abraham was in his time. The question is whether to believe God's Word, the Bible. It makes no difference whether His message is written or spoken. The important thing was that Abraham recognized the source of the message and was willing to obey it.

More important than Abraham's progeny was his fathering a people who would follow in his footsteps of faith. He was, in effect, to start the faith race. Such a race consists of people who would be distinctive in that they would be able to understand spiritual matters as Abraham did. At the start, being Jewish wasn't just a matter of genealogy; it depended on a person's relationship with God.

Abraham had two sons, Ishmael and Isaac. Isaac was a man of faith. It was through him that the faith race was to continue. Similarly, Isaac had two sons, Esau and Jacob. But Esau was not interested in spiritual matters. So it was to be through Jacob that the blessing would continue. You see the pattern. Those who followed after God in faith received spiritual blessing.

The faith these men had was not in positive thinking. They didn't put their confidence in mind over matter, self-hypnosis, or in anything other than God. They knew He would not break His Word.

Faith must be placed in the right thing. Faith that planting stones in the ground would produce trees would be a faulty faith. Obviously Abraham's faith was successful because he had faith in the right thing—God's Word. This wisdom was passed on. Thus, Abraham started a faith race as well as a physical one. All those who believed, as Abraham did, could rightfully make claim to the spiritual promises made to Abraham.

Abraham's faith race was promised blessing to all who were born of God's Spirit. But Abraham also had certain promises made to his physical "seed." Anyone who doubts this need only look to the eternal promises given to Jews concerning the land of Israel. There also were promises given to the Arab nations for they, too, are descendents of Abraham. God's Word is valid on a spiritual as well as a physical plane.

On a physical level, God made some promises to the "seed" of Abraham, Isaac and Jacob which were not made to all peoples. Their descendents were to have a special historical purpose. Through the Jews, many nations have been blessed with a system of laws and social order, to say nothing of scientific and business skills.

Some people might mistakenly classify Messianic Judaism as just another Christian denomination. It is not. The distinctive function of the Jew has been God-ordained. All other denominational differences were made by theologians. Such man-made denominational distinctions cannot be found anywhere in the Bible. But Jewish distinctiveness can be found there. The church gradually is becoming more aware of this.

The New Covenant explains that Gentiles need to become part of the natural olive tree (faith race). Just because there has been a lot of grafting of the wild olive branches does not mean that the natural branches should be forced to deny their natural origin. Better the wild olive branches should become more conformed to the natural tree. Are Gentile believers really pleased that they have been grafted into the olive tree? Or, has the church been insisting that the natural olive branches become part of the wild branch (Gentiles)?

For nearly 2,000 years, Gentiles have acted as though it was Jews who must become part of the Gentile faith. This is contrary to the plan in the Bible. Actually, non-believing Gentiles become converted to biblical Judaism when they become believers. Non-believing Jews become reimplanted when they rediscover the faith of their forefathers.

Jewish non-believers have become more aware of the seeming emptiness and purposeless of this atheistic age. Many such Jews are asking themselves why Yeshua isn't considered the Jewish Messiah. They no longer are satisfied with a policy decision made thousands of years ago by some unfamiliar ancestor.

Discussion of the true Jewish faith is distressing to the rabbinical community, since it brings into question the basis by which one qualifies as a Jew. The dispersion proved the Jewish faith simply isn't a matter of nationality or language. The Bible shows it strictly isn't a matter of physical lineage, either. In the Old Covenant, many non-Jews were brought into the faith. Also, many of Hebrew descent were not considered part of the household of Israel, since they were not of the faith. The same criteria should apply today. Real Jews should be spiritually minded as were the founders of the faith.

Today, Rabbinical Judaism can't agree on what it is in favor of; it only agrees on what it's against. In the eyes of Rabbis, a person of Jewish descent is required to be against Christ. Yet what did He do to arouse such animosity? Isn't is about time the Rabbis got down to the heart of the issue. For openers, why not define a Jew as a member of a people who have a covenant with God through Abraham, Moses and David?

Biblical students know that the evangelical Christian belief that being lost until saved is an Old Testament concept in accordance with Isaiah 53:6. Rabbinical leaders owe it to the Jewish people to articulate why they believe Yeshua isn't the Messiah. A case against Him has not been made after nearly 2,000 years of trying.

Jews are becoming more aware of this and are looking at the New Covenant with renewed interest. What's more, Messianic Judaism may be the means by which the wall between Jew and Christian is finally broken down. Who can deny the close spiritual relationship between people who have the bond of a personal encounter with the Messiah?

Up to this point, the Christian community has said Jews should come over to their side of the wall, convert, ignore everything that is Jewish and the wall of partition no longer will be a problem. Everyone would be on the same side of the wall.

Jews have been saying the same thing in reverse. They contend that Christians have an unintelligent religion based on idolatry and fairy tales. Jews say come over to their way of thinking and all will be unified.

In either case, the wall of partition still stands. Both groups are asking each other to yield. That's the rub; neither side will.

The true Christian who has had a spiritual experience would not want to return to a one-way conversation with God. The Jew, on the other hand, does not want to become a Gentile. It is abhorrent to him to become part of something which has brought so much agony to him and his ancestors. Moreover, Christianity appears illogical to a Jew. He assumes that since he can't understand it, no logical person could. This is a common error among all unbelievers who try to understand faith through intellect. They do not understand that there are three parts to a person—a physical body, a soul (mind), and a spirit.

Everyone is familiar with what the body is. They are less certain of how the mind works. But most people don't even know their spirit exists, let alone understand how it works. It is the least tangible part of a person. But it probably is the most valuable since it continues to exist forever.

The reason most people are unaware of their spirit is because it isn't functioning. Their spirit is submerged beneath their intellect and emotion. When reasoning so dominates spiritual insight, the spirit ceases to function. For all practical purposes, it is dead. It needs to be rejuvenated. It is important to see how man's spirit got into this condition. Then he will understand how to achieve the needed rejuvenation.

Originally, Adam and Eve were in perfect fellowship with God. But they chose to believe Satan's false promises.

True to form, Satan lied. He said if you wrench some knowledge of how things work from the forbidden tree, you can be equal to God. At this point, the first two persons on earth faced a moral decision—whether to believe God or Satan. Adam and Eve believed Satan's lie. They took the fruit from the tree of knowledge, but they didn't become God's equal. All they got was trouble. Because of their transgression, they were separated from God. To deal with their difficulties, they depended upon their intellect. This, in turn, separated them even further from God. Thus, they increasingly used their intellect and emotion and exercised less and less faith.

This has been mankind's condition for many centuries. Satan had proved himself stronger than man. Yet man had the promise that someday a Messiah would come who was stronger than Satan. Such a man was the carpenter from Galilee. He took the worst that Satan could muster and defeated him.

He chose to let Himself be sacrificed, taking the penalty due us so we could be in right standing before God. Just as one man, Adam, got us into a mess, another man, Yeshua, could get us out.

Adam's weakness sent man far from his peaceful home. Messiah's strength is the means of returning. The choice of humanity is whether Adam or Yeshua will be the captain of its faith. Whose faith will they follow, Adam's or the Messiah's? In whose footsteps do they want to follow?

Once mankind recognized what happened on the cross (tree), it can have confidence that Satan can be beaten. If one man can defeat Satan, the rest of us can step over him. Man has his big brother, Yeshua, to call upon for help. Once this is accepted, regret over past failures can be expressed freely to the Lord. Acceptance of the Messiah through our eyes of faith can now regain its original dominance over the physical senses. Then fellowship with the Lord is possible again.

We can see that being a member of God's family has nothing to do with our biology or affiliation with a particular church or synagogue. For spiritual birth, mankind needs to be at one with the Father of all spirits. This comes through repentance and belief that the Messiah's sacrificial blood did it all. This needs to be explained to non-believing Jews and Gentiles alike.

Once a person's spiritual side has been rejuvenated, their spirit works in cooperation with the Holy Spirit of God. When human spirits cooperate with the Spirit of the Great Harmonizer, they are cooperating with one another. Then Jew and Gentile are one in the Spirit.

Most people have not rejected spiritual rebirth, they simply never heard of it. Similarly, most Jews have not rejected the Messiah, they simply don't know or understand Him. This is because of the false image of Christianity presented by those who have not been born of the spirit.

For nearly 2,000 years, there has been an unnecessary breach between Jew and Gentile. Neither has shown much interest in tearing down this barrier. Now, Messianic Judaism provides a middle ground for accomplishing what cannot be done by coercion.

In a sense, Messianic Judaism says that believing Christians can enjoy a fuller, richer faith as they see it in its original context. Similarly, Jews can see the peace and joy available to them, while still being Jewish. What reasonable person wouldn't want to have a personal relationship with the God of Abraham, Isaac and Jacob, especially since it can be had without abandoning a rich heritage?

In time, both groups will come to appreciate what is available from the other. Messianic Gentiles will want to enjoy the richness of Judaism, and Jews will come into greater appreciation of the wisdom of the New Covenant. Then Jew and Gentile truly can be one in the Spirit.

Now, of course, God still has different purposes for

different people in the physical realm. Although hands and feet have different functions, they still are part of the same body. People should look forward to the day when Christians will be grateful to Jews for bringing the Word of God, and Jews will appreciate Christians for showing them the fulfillment of their Judaism.

Perhaps some will not be able to understand Messianic Judaism immediately. Christians might mistakenly accuse completed Jews of trying to Judaize believers. Such a contention would be wrong. There were Jews in Galatia 1,900 years ago who insisted that Gentiles must observe the outward forms of synagogue worship. They were trying to make Jewish rituals a requirement for salvation.

Judged by outward appearances, it might seem that Messianic Jews are insisting on the same thing today. This is not the case. Completed Jews participate in such observances as a matter of preference, not because it is required. Moreover, these observances do not help anyone get to heaven. They merely are a chosen form of expression which isn't forced on anyone. God is concerned with the motivations of the heart.

Messianic Jews realize that the Mosaic Law was the means by which God showed the impossibility of human nature living up to His standards. But when God reveals Himself, He softens the heart. This makes it easier to do His will. When this happens, people shed more of their human nature and become more conformed to God's loving nature. Then God's laws are no longer written on stone tablets, but on the fleshy tablets of human hearts.

Once Yeshua fulfilled all the symbolic foreshadowing of the Mosaic Code, it no longer was the mainspring of the Messianic faith. Who needs a shadow when they can have the substance—The Messiah Himself?

Within the Mosaic Law there are instructions to observe various feasts forever. All believers do observe these holidays when they celebrate the Messiah. He is their Passover, He is their Pentecost. He fulfilled their Day of Atonement, and believers will dwell in His Tabernacles forever, for these holy days will last eternally. Yeshua fulfilled the law by His actions, and He became the embodiment of God's law. Maintaining Jewish identity is consistent with Scripture.

This also is helpful when discussing spiritual matters with relatives and friends. It is ironic that well-meaning true Christians label Judaizing a taboo, then fall into the same trap themselves. Christians might reflect on how obviously correct Saul (Paul) was to remove such obstacles to prospective Gentile believers. After all, such ceremonies and symbols were extremely foreign and meaningless to a Greek. What wisdom it was for Paul to see that nothing should stand in the way of a person's understanding of the Messianic concepts, and that insistence on such obstacles actually were thwarting the Holy Spirit.

Yet this same situation exists today—in reverse this time. It is called Gentilizing. Some 2,000 years ago, it was Jews who were the custodians of God's Truth. Some Jews erred by insisting that Gentiles should conform to many of their traditions, customs and institutions. They were, in a sense, insisting that Gentiles become appendages of already established synagogue institutions.

Some Gentile churches today insist that when Jews become believers they must become Gentiles, attend established churches, and observe Gentile rituals that are foreign to their Hebrew heritage. Don't we have modern day Pharisees possessive of their Savior and claim He only belongs to the Gentiles? In effect, Gentiles are insisting that Jews enter the faith only through the regular church establishment. Isn't bringing God's Word to the house of Israel of overriding importance?

What procedure would Rabbi Saul advise? He probably would suggest what he did under similar circumstances—

not let these cultural differences become a stumbling block which prevents a person from coming into a right standing relationship with God. The form is secondary to the substance. Paul wanted to be all things to all men so that some might be more willing to look at the Truth.

IX
A JEW TO THE JEWS

Why do Jews become the disciples of Yeshua? In past centuries traditional Judaism had only one answer: for material gain. As for those Jews who already were well-off financially, it was interpreted as a desire to escape their Jewishness and assimilate. This really does not explain why first century Jews became followers.

Since it was intolerable from the rabbinical viewpoint that Jewish believers acted out of pure conviction, other rationalizations were used—alienation from Judaism or lack of Jewish background, for example.

The alienation theory was untrue then, and it still is. Today's Messianic Jews prove by practice that they are more Jewish than ever before. The other rabbinical explanation that lack of Jewish education opened the door to Christian evangelism is another unproved assumption.

To combat all this, rabbinical strategy has been to offer heavy doses of Jewish culture. But Jewish culture without God is powerless.

The overall goal today is to infuse Jewish youth with a greater sense of racial pride. By doing so, Jewish leaders hope to make young Jews immune to evangelistic outreach. The Rabbis do not realize that evangelism is addressed to people who have not yet been born of the Spirit. This includes Jews, Catholics, Protestants and others of all denominations. This strategy shows a lack of understanding when it is considered that completed Jews aggressively try to learn more about their Jewish heritage after coming to know the Lord.

Such sociological explanations will not do. The real answers are in the spiritual realm. Perhaps the Rabbis should consider the explanation offered by completed Jews themselves. They would be told it is knowing God that motivates them.

A Gallup Poll showed that non-Jews believing in God with "absolute certainty" ranged between 73 and 88 percent. Only 39 percent of Jews interviewed expressed similar conviction. How pale this seems when compared with the certainty of Messianic Jews that God exists. Why else would a Jew undergo so much criticism and ostracism?

The traditional branches of Judaism—Orthodox, Reformed and Conservative—do not offer a truly satisfying experience for completed Jews. The Orthodox believe in an ethical God who has provided literal instruction (without apparent meaning). Their theology is that a person should seek to have his good deeds outweigh his bad ones and thereby achieve everlasting life. The Messianic Jew finds that achieving heaven through good deeds to be inconsistent with the Old Testament prophet Isaiah, who said, "all of our righteousnesses are as filthy rags."

The Reformed are a much larger group and more liberal. It is a religion of personal opinion. Although there are remnants of the Orthodox ritual, the individual is free to accept or reject biblical precepts. Messianic Jews place more emphasis on the Scriptures than on Biblical commentaries. In troubled times Jewish culture is not much comfort. It appears to be a hollow means of seeking the Almighty.

Conversative Judaism seeks a middle ground between the other two. Some of the Hebrew language has been translated and the services have been modernized to some extent. Thus, Conservative Judaism tries to adapt to its environment. Since the Messianic Jew seeks a more biblical Judaism, a middle ground between either of the above still does not fully satisfy his needs.

Reconstructionism is the most recent novelty among Jews. Its emphasis is on the Jewish community. Since its adherents are not interested in religion, it is regarded by Messianic Jews as one of the last stages of complete abandonment of Jewishness. It is not even considered a religious branch by completed Jews.

The establishment church also has taken note of the new Jew. One significance of these developments is that the New Covenant message still speaks to those to whom it was originally addressed. Another significance is that Jewish believers can bring a new perspective to an age-old controversy.

As previously mentioned, there now is a real opportunity to break down the middle wall of partition (Ephesians 2:14-22). In this way, in Spirit there will be neither Jew nor Greek (Galatians 3:22-29). Although this should serve as an advantage to both, misunderstanding is possible. This would be destructive to the desire for all to be part of one body (Ephesians 4:3-6).

Paul saw no inconsistency between being a part of this body and being Jewish, as he always had been. He attempted to break down the middle wall of partition by promoting the idea that a person could remain either a Jew or a Gentile. He applied it to himself. He referred to himself as a Jew, not a former Jew (Acts 22:3). He also considered himself a Pharisee, not a former Pharisee (Acts 23:6). Paul further identified himself as being of Israel (Romans 11:1). He did not say he formerly was of Israel. In II Corinthians 11:22, this same apostle called himself a Hebrew, not a former Hebrew. In each case he went out of his way to show both Jew and Gentile he still considered himself part and parcel of the household of Israel.

Without Paul, the Gentiles might never have known the Messiah. The church, then, should heed Paul. He insisted on being a Jew. He also described his role toward other Jews. He said he would be a Jew to the Jews (I Corinthians 9:20, 10:31-33). He did this to help save souls. As a Jew, he was fulfilling the great commandment to spread the good news throughout the world; to the Jew first, and also to the Greek.

In many ways, the institutional church has not fulfilled its mission of presenting the good news of the Messiah to the Jewish people. As servants of God, a choice must be made between the esteem of men or the friendship of God.

One indication that biblical Judaism is in God's plan is that Jewish people are more open to what He has to say when they believe it is not contrary to the true Judaism practiced by their ancestors.

Now, more than ever before, Jewish people are feeling the emptiness of a spiritual vacuum. Only God can fill it. Especially in this age of skepticism, Jews are too intelligent to think that lighting candles and Jewish culture alone can fill the void of a meaningless existence. Customs and traditions are valuable, of course, but they must be motivated by a desire to please God. When the heart is right, the ceremony is right.

If mainstream Judaism is to accept a Jewish Messiah, it will not be accomplished in an institutional church. For one thing, it is difficult to get a Jewish person to even visit a church. When he does, he sees symbols, statues and ornaments that are foreign to him. Also, he is likely to be a numerical minority and subject to the direction of non-Jewish church leaders who might find it difficult to cater to his sense of Jewish identity.

Moreover, most Gentiles do not recognize the full importance of their Jewish roots. Typically, well-meaning Christians want their Jewish friends to become part of the local church. But chances are Jews aren't buying it. Wouldn't Jews be more willing to listen if it were understood that the Gentile Christian is participating in something genuinely Hebrew.

But how can he hear the good news about the Jewish Messiah if he isn't exposed to it? God has created Messianic synagogues for such a circumstance as this. Both Jews and Christians attend their services. The average Jewish person might come to a Messianic congregation, despite his unwillingness to go to a church. There he is in familiar surroundings and he can see services enjoyed by many Jewish people.

The words "church" and "synagogue" simply mean a congregation gathered for worship. Whether or not such worship is of God is an individual thing. Motivation when attending them is of supreme importance.

Since Jews normally attend synagogues, the surroundings are more familiar and it is credible that acceptance of biblical doctrines of the New Covenant is a Jewish thing to do. And since a cross has been the symbol of Jewish persecution for so long, Messianic congregations do not display one. Instead of making it an issue, such congregations display symbols that are familiar and scripturally correct. This eliminated much of the discomfort.

With trappings and terminology no longer a problem and Jewish people present, the inquiring Jewish person can now address his attention to the main issues. Thus, he is hopefully now weighing the doctrines of Scripture with an open mind, rather than assuming they are Gentile concepts. In this way, the Bible is receiving a fair hearing. The logic of the case must be considered, rather than some distracting issue.

People cannot help but notice the Spirit of God and His love present at such services. In this way, Jew and Gentile can worship together as children of the same God. After a person has accepted Messiah Yeshua, he is encouraged to obtain regular spiritual fellowship at a place where there is a spirit of grace and supplication to the Lord. Perhaps, this could be at a Messianic synagogue.

The New Covenant refers to synagogues of Satan (Revelations 2:9, 3:9). Isn't it possible for a synagogue to glorify God? The Messiah and his disciples, for example, attended synagogues. Anyone critical of synagogues should remember that they predate churches.

Luke 7:2-5 tells of a Roman centurion who was held in high esteem by early followers of the Messiah because he had built a synagogue for them. Yeshua must have had similar appreciation since He was willing to go to the centurion's home to heal an ailing servant. Yeshua was not displeased because the centurion built a synagogue rather than a church. Instead, it was a point to the centurion's credit.

The Scriptures clearly establish that this centurion was a man of faith. He sent his friends to the Messiah to save Him a journey. The centurion said he understood authority and, therefore, knew Yeshua didn't have to be physically present and could heal by remote control. Does this centurion sound like an evil person? No indeed! Did Yeshua find fault with him for building a Jewish synagogue? Certainly not! This centurion was considered among the most faithful in all Israel (Matthew 8:10).

Today, the world is in need of more believers like this centurion. Participating in the building of synagogues not only showed a willingness to help Jews, it also was an act of great faith. For out of the mustard seed, Messianic synagogues can grow which will help clarify a 2,000-year-old misunderstanding.

Above all, Messianic congregations are part of the body of the Messiah. But not all of the body functions the same. Eyes can't hear and ears can't see. Since God has provided Jews with a desire to be born a Jew and die a Jew, let them.

When the Messiah was called a Jew by the Samaritan woman in John 4:22, He neither denied nor objected to this designation. The Messiah was born a Jew and wanted to die a Jew. Why shouldn't everyone be permitted to attend a synagogue the way the Messiah did?

One natural extension of the synagogue concept is the celebration of Jewish holy days. Passover, Shavuot, Sukkot, Purim, Hanukkah, the Feast of Trumpets and Day of Atonement are wonderful occasions to obtain Biblical insights.

X

THE HIGHER MEANING OF
JEWISH HOLIDAYS

People often forget the word "holiday" is derived from "holy day." In many ways these solemn assemblies have lost much of their original meaning.

By celebrating these holy convocations, Messianic synagogues not only can observe them in the traditional sense, but the New Covenant also gives them a higher meaning. Thus, otherwise meaningless ritual can be seen as a foreshadowing of future events.

PASSOVER

Exodus 12 gives a full description of the first Passover and its observance is commanded in Leviticus 23:5-7. According to these instructions the first and last days of this seven-day convocation were to be considered holy. Unleavened bread was to be eaten during this period. Traditionally, this was to commemorate the exodus of Israelites from Egypt. They were so rushed they were unable to wait for the yeast to rise in the bread they were baking. Today, bread eaten on this holiday must be unleavened (matzah).

In the New Covenant, the Messiah compared Himself with this bread when He celebrated the Passover. The parallels are worth noting. Yeast is a symbol of sin. It swells, ferments and decays. The Messiah was not puffed up; neither was the matzah. Both have holes from having been pierced. The stripes on the matzah are reminders of the stripes on the Messiah's back from the whippings he suffered. During the Passover Seder (supper), three pieces of matzah were placed in. a cloth. The middle piece was broken, as was the Messiah's body. Half of the matzah is hidden and awaits discovery. Isn't this how it is with the Messiah? Anyone truly seeking Him will find Him. The middle piece is called the *Afikomen*. *Afikomenos* in Greek means "I have come." It also means "I will return."

When Yeshua dipped the sop and gave it to Judas, He actually was participating in an ancient Passover tradition of dipping greens or parsley into salt water. This has been done for some 3,500 years; it is called the "Karpas" ceremony. Traditionally it represents the hyssop dipped into the blood basin in Egypt and applied to the door post and lintel.

One of the Hallel Psalms sung on this holiday is Psalms 118:22-29. One line of it says: "The stone which the builders refused is become the head stone of the corner." How true. The psalmist foresaw a thousand years before the event that the cornerstone of the Jewish faith was to be refused by the builders of the faith (Jews). Since the Messiah was to become the cornerstone of the faith, He also was to become the basis on which everything else derives its meaning. A strong cornerstone is the foundation of a solid structure. It is recorded in the New Covenant that after a particular Passover Seder (the Last Supper) they sang the traditional Hallel psalms.

During the Last Supper, Yeshua took a cup of wine. In a traditional Seder, four cups of wine are taken. The Messiah compared His blood to the wine. As He took the cup, He was accepting His fate. He also knew He was signing his own death warrant. He had accepted the will of the Father in order to reconcile the world.

As in other wills, there are no beneficiaries until someone dies. The New Testament (New Will) wasn't sealed until Yeshua's death. Yeshua indirectly was saying to Judas: they can come and take me now. Yeshua said He wouldn't drink of the wine again with His followers until He could enjoy it with them in heaven.

Another biblical symbol is the pascal lamb. The shank bone of a lamb is displayed at the Seder. As you will remember from the Passover story, God said:

> "Yet will I bring one plague more upon Pharaoh and upon Egypt; afterwards he will let you go hence ... About midnight will I go out into the midst of Egypt: And all the first-born of the land of Egypt shall die ... they shall take to them every man a lamb . . . your lamb shall be without blemish ... and they shall take of the blood and strike in on the two side posts and on the upper door posts of the houses ... and when I see the blood, I will pass over you, and the plague shall not be upon you to destroy you, when I smite the land of Egypt" (Exodus 11,12).

Note that the blood of this lamb was to be applied to the upper door (lintel) and to the two side posts. Even the blood was required for deliverance from the death angel. How much like a lamb was the Messiah. He was meek like a lamb and He offered no resistance.

Bethlehem, where Yeshua was born, was the city in which sacrificial lambs were raised. He was sacrificed at Passover time. His Last Supper was a Passover Seder. Even the commemoration of His Last Supper is really a miniature Passover Seder.

Traditional observance of this occasion by Jews should be called the feast of the "unleavened bread" because there is no passover lamb present, no sacrifice, and no blood of atonement. However, practices such as reclining on a couch, the kittel (white gown), and the four cups of wine have no special merit in God's sight, since they merely were embellishments added by Rabbis.

SHAVUOT

The Jewish custom of counting seven weeks from Passover is based on the commandment given in Leviticus 23: 15-21:

> "And ye shall count unto you from the morrow after the sabbath, from the day that ye brought the sheaf of the wave offering: seven sabbaths shall be complete: Even unto the morrow after the seventh sabbath shall ye number fifty days; and ye shall offer a new meal offering unto the Lord. Ye shall bring out of your habitations two wave-loaves ... they shall be of fine flour; they shall be baken with leaven; they are the first fruits unto the Lord ... And ye shall proclaim on the self-same day, that it may be an holy convocation unto you: ye shall do not servile work therein: it shall be a statute for ever in all your dwellings throughout your generations."

Thus, from the second morning of Passover, Jews were to count 49 days. The 50th day was to be Shavuot. This holiday also is referred to as the festival of the Wheat Harvest, or the Day of the First Fruits.

On Shavuot (Pentecost), two loaves made of fine flour and baked with leaven were waved before the Lord. One can see the significance of this, since it symbolizes both the Jew and Gentile, which comprise the aggregate body of the Messiah. The Book of Ruth is read on this occasion since it tells of the harvest and demonstrates how Ruth, a Moabite, became part of the Jewish people by faith.

In Deuteronomy 16:9-12, 16 and 17, it is shown that this was a time for a sacrificial offering to the Lord according to how each man prospered. This always was a harvest time full of rejoicing. Exodus 34:22-24 and Numbers 28:26-31 also refer to Shavuot.

Of course Paul, while being an apostle to the Gentiles, also observed Jewish traditions. For example, he wanted to be in Jerusalem to celebrate this holiday (Acts 20:16). Before the Jewish people were dispersed, Shavuot was a popular holiday. After the scattering, however, the holiday's primary emphasis was diminished as a harvest festival. It came to commemorate the giving of the law to Moses. By rabbinical calculation, it was given to Moses on Shavuot.

It was on Shavuot that the disciples of Yeshua were gathered in an upper room in Jerusalem waiting for the return of the Lord. The Holy Spirit of God descended upon them, giving them power to announce good news about the Messiah. The good news was that He overcame Satan, conquered death, and arose on the third day. This power manifested itself in many miraculous gifts which were evidences of God's supernatural workings among men. As in the first century, the church is showing renewed interest in God's supernatural power. It is clear that God was pouring out His Holy Spirit and has accelerated the harvest of souls. Hence, a spiritual counterpart to the harvest holiday of Shavuot is seen.

FEAST OF TRUMPETS

Rabbis sought to make a calendar adjustment to compensate for the differences in the lunar year, and place the start of a new year at the beginning of the seventh month of Tishri instead of at Passover as the Bible commands. Despite the clear biblical statement that Nisan (Passover time is in the spring) "shall be the beginning of months" (Exodus 12:2), traditional Judaism mistakenly celebrates the New Year in the seventh month (Tishri) and calls it Rosh Hashana.

The Bible suggests that a holy celebration be held in the month of Tishri. This is the Feast of Trumpets.

> "In the seventh month, the first day of the month, shall ye have a sabbath a memorial of blowing of trumpets, a holy convocation" (Leviticus 23:21).

The observance of this holy day is mentioned in Nehemiah 8:1-12, where the Law was read to Jewish people who had returned from Babylonian captivity on the Feast of Trumpets.

The sounding of the shofar (ram's horn) mentioned in the Bible was done to call an assembly, sound an alarm, or to commemorate a memorial before God. Joel 2:12-15 says it is a call to repentance.

YOM KIPPUR

This holiday is celebrated 10 days after Rosh Hashana. Literally translated it means "Day of Atonement." Leviticus 23:26-32 tells Jews to observe the day of atonement. It is a day in which the Jewish nation afflicts its soul with anguish. Kippur means "covering" as in covering blood (atonement). It also is found in Psalm 78:38. God said when He sees the blood he would pass over.

According to Leviticus 17:11, it is the "blood that maketh an atonement for the soul." Without sacrificial blood there is no remission of sins. Thus, there cannot be a real day of atonement until Jews accept the vicarious sacrifice of righteous blood which only the Messiah can make. Since the Temple had been destroyed, only His sacrifice would satisfy God's requirements. Thus, blood is the covering for repentant believers. When God sees the blood He passes over it and doesn't see the sin under it.

Traditional Judaism substitutes prayer and charity for the blood. It is hoped that good deeds outweigh bad ones. This line of thought was developed by the Rabbis to deal with the dilemma facing traditional Jews. The dilemma was that the Bible says Jews need to make sacrifices in the Temple, but the Temple no longer stands. This is a common sense solution, but it doesn't satisfy God. The Bible says "all of our righteousnesses are as filthy rags."

Leviticus 16 tells the procedure for sacrifice. Leviticus 17 discusses blood, not charity or good deeds. Who would want to trust atonement to the opinion of some ancient Rabbis they never met? Isn't it better to lean on God's everlasting Word?

On this holy day the Rabbis tells us to fast. To traditional Jews, this is the day to plead with God for forgiveness. When the day is over, no one knows whether they have been forgiven.

The Messianic Jew has atonement every moment of his life. He has an infinite sacrifice available to him for his crimes against the Almighty. What's more, he has an absolute knowledge of forgiveness. God promised it in His Word. "God is not a man that he should lie" (Numbers 23:19). He doesn't make mistakes and He doesn't have to yield to anyone. Either all of God's Word is true or none of it is.

SUKKOT

This holiday also is referred to as the Feast of Tabernacles (portable house of worship, easily constructed). It is an observance ordered in Leviticus 23:33-43.

> "The fifteenth day of this seventh month shall be the feast of tabernacles for seven days unto the Lord. On the first day shall be an holy convocation; ye shall do no servile work therein. Seven days ye shall offer an offering made by fire unto the Lord ... when ye have gathered in the fruit of the land, ye shall keep a feast unto the Lord seven days; on the first day shall be a sabbath, and on the eighth day shall be a sabbath. And ye shall take you on the first day and boughs of goodly trees, branches of palm trees, and the boughs of thick trees, and willows of the brook; and ye shall rejoice before the Lord your God seven days . . . It shall be a statute forever in your generation ... Ye shall dwell in booths seven days; all that are Israelites born shall dwell in booths; That your generations may know that I made the children of Israel to dwell in booths, when I brought them out of the land of Egypt ..."

It essentially is a harvest festival and a time of rejoicing The holiday commemorates God's faithfulness in providing for the Jewish people when He brought them out of Egypt. It is one of three times during the year when all men had to appear before the Lord in Jerusalem. The others were Passover and Shavuot (Deuteronomy 16:16,17; Exodus 23:14-19, and Exodus 34:22-26). Sukkot also is observed in Ezra 3:4 and Nehemiah 8:13-18.

On this holiday a lulav made of branches of palms and willows fastened with golden thread is waved and Psalms 113-118 are sung. This traditionally symbolizes God's sovereignty over the entire world. An etrog (citrus similar to a lemon) symbolic of the fruit of the autumn harvest is used. In synagogue worship the lulav, the etrog, three myrtle branches and two willow branches are carried and the congregation sings Hosanna, which means "save us" or "save now."

The New Covenant adds additional dimension to the Holy Day. The pouring of the water during the service is symbolic of the living waters promised to all who accept the Messiah. It is the living waters that satisfy spiritual thirst. When the Messiah returns to set up His kingdom, all nations will come to Jerusalem to keep the Feast of the Tabernacles.

> "And it shall come to pass that everyone that is left of all the nations which came against Jerusalem shall even go up from year to year to worship the King, the Lord of hosts and to keep the feast of tabernacles. And it shall be, that whosoever will not come up of all the families of the earth unto Jerusalem to worship the King, the Lord of hosts, even upon them shall be no rain. And if the family of Egypt go not up, and come not, that have no rain, there shall be the plague, where with the Lord will smite the heathen that come not to keep the feast of tabernacles. This shall be the punishment of Egypt, and the punishment of all nations that come not up to keep the feast of tabernacles" (Zechariah 14:16-19).

Often it seems that the church believes that the Messiah came to destroy the laws concerning the holidays. He said He did not come to overturn the law, but to fulfill it. In the future, all nations will want to celebrate Sukkot. They will recognize that it is in their best interest if they wish to have good harvests. People do not have to keep God's edicts. It's just that things go better when they do. The world will eventually realize this. Then it will have a Messianic age.

HANUKKAH

Hanukkah sometimes is referred to as the Feast of Lights. The only biblical reference to it is in the New Covenant, where it says the Messiah celebrated it. It is not considered a really important holiday, but it occurs about Christmas time. For this reason, modern western culture has elevated its importance.

It commemorates a time when Jews were under a Syrian king, Antiochus, who had erected an altar to Zeus. Mattathias, a Jewish priest, refused to acknowledge the preeminence of this false god. Eventually, it resulted in the revolt of the Maccabees. Mattathias and his five sons took to the hills and engaged in guerilla warfare against the Syrians. A year later in 167 B.C., Mattathias relinquished the revolt's leadership to his son Judah, nicknamed "the hammer." Judah, the Maccabee, was a brilliant tactician and a master of the surprise attack. After much fasting, prayer and heroism, the Maccabees prevailed and the Syrians fled.

The Temple was rededicated on the twenty-fifth day of Kislev (December) in 165 B.C. In order to light the Temple, a search was made for consecrated oil. Only one container of such oil could be found. Yet it lasted eight days. This is recorded in the rabbinical commentary of the Talmud.

The celebration is a time of praise and thanksgiving to God. It is a secular occasion rather than a holy day. Traditionally, there are latkes (potato pancakes), gifts and games for children using dreydles (tops).

Celebrated as a Feast of Lights, it reminds one of a biblical analogy. The Messiah said that He was the light of the world and that anyone who would follow Him would not have the darkness of confusion, but would have the light of understanding. He also said that believers are the light of the world. He advised His followers to share this understanding with others.

PURIM

King Ahasuerus of Persia was offended by his queen, Vashti, and set about to find another wife. In the city of Shushan, a Jew named Mordecai was the uncle of a beautiful maiden named Esther. The king met and fell in love with her and she became queen of all Persia.

Since she usually was secluded, Queen Esther rarely could communicate with her uncle who sat at the city gate hoping for a glimpse of her. One day Mordecai heard two palace gatekeepers plotting against the king. He sent a message to Esther. The gatekeepers were tried and hanged and Mordecai's patriotism was recorded in the king's Great Book of Deeds.

Shortly afterward, an evil man, Haman, was appointed to a position of great power within the palace. Mordecai refused to bow to him and Haman decided all Jews in Persia should die for this disrespect. The king agreed.

Esther saw the sorrow and fear this decision created among her people. Her uncle said to her, ". . who knoweth whether thou art come to the kingdom for such a time as this" (Esther 4:14). Although approaching the king unsummoned was not permitted, Esther was determined to make a direct appeal to him. If he was displeased, she would surely die. The king did not rebuke her for her boldness and asked her to make a request. He said she could request up to half his kingdom. She asked that Haman be invited to a banquet. Haman was greatly pleased at this honor. His ego swelled, and more than ever he wanted Mordecai to bow before him. When Mordecai still would not bow, Haman decided to build a gallows for him.

During the banquet Esther told the king of an enemy of her people. She revealed Haman's plan to kill Mordecai, despite his earlier service and loyalty to the king. King Ahasuerus decided to hang Haman instead, and Esther's people were saved.

Since then, Purim has been celebrated with the telling of this event in the Megilla, a scroll of the Book of Esther. Throughout the tale there is much cheering of Mordecai and booing of Haman.

In this story one can see the Lord's hand moving. Indeed Providence had arranged fortuitous circumstances. Consider for a moment Esther's beauty and her selection as queen, Mordecai's service to the king and the recording of it in the king's Great Book of Deeds. It all was arranged by the Almighty. Esther is a true Bible heroine. She could have lived out her life in comfort without concern for her people. As queen she could have easily rationalized that it was not her position to intrude in the intricacies of politics. Instead, she decided to stand up for her people. It is possible that she, too, could have been included in the mass murder planned by Haman.

Commemoration of Purim is more than hamentashens (cakes) and groggers (noisemakers). It contains spiritual principles because loyalty and service to our king will be recorded in God's Book of Great Deeds. These won't get us into heaven, but we will receive our reward. The law of reaping and sowing never has been repealed. More importantly, believers are written in the Lamb's Book of Life, based on the Messiah's righteousness, not on ours.

XI
THE MERCY OF THE GENTILES

The Gentile world entered the faith race largely through the merciful efforts of Paul and Jews of similar persuasion. He was willing to endure great hardship in order to bring an important message to the world. In Paul's time, most Jews felt that Gentiles should accept Jewish laws, customs and traditions in order to become part of the true faith.

Paul's doctrine was revolutionary. He said that although such observances were desirable and commendable, they were not necessary to achieve fellowship with God. He said it was more important that the Gentiles receive the Lord than to worry about technicalities in the Mosaic Law. If such observances were stumbling blocks, he suggested that they be discarded.

It was not easy for Paul to risk being called a heretic in order to reach the Gentiles. But Paul was God's man and he had compassion for these foreign peoples. He and men like him went through great suffering and ostracism so that the Gentile world might know of the Good Shepherd who laid down His life for His sheep.

Eventually Messianic Jews, who were zealous of the law, permitted non-Jews to enter the community of believers in Jerusalem, thus becoming Jews. It is somewhat paradoxical that the progeny of those who benefited from the mercy of Paul and other Jews, now are called upon to show similar mercy. Now, as then, there will be controversy. Perhaps some may seek to redefine New Testament faith so that there will be no room for Jews who show respect for the Mosaic Code. In effect, such legalistic believers will themselves be setting up a law preventing anyone from observing the statutes of the Bible.

Such new legalism would be just as deadly as the first. Nowhere in the Bible does it say that a Jew is prevented from observing Jewish rites commanded in the Old Testament. The New Covenant simply says it is not mandatory to obtain salvation. Just because it is not critical does not mean it is a sin. Nevertheless, God prefers obedience more than sacrifice (I Samuel 15:22). This means He would prefer that mankind obey His will, rather than have to apply the blood of atonement.

Paul was a bold apostle, but not the only apostle. Peter and James were apostles to the Jews. They lived according to the law of the Torah (five books giving 613 laws of Moses) and encouraged belief in Yeshua among their own people who, because they were Jews, had a lifestyle peculiar to their culture. Paul, Barnabas and Silas, as apostles to the Gentiles, encouraged belief in Yeshua to peoples who found Jewish lifestyle burdensome. Today, Gentiles should recognize that simply because they find Jewish lifestyle uninteresting is no reason to assume it is dull to a Jew.

If non-Jews don't wish to accept Jewish culture as mandatory, is it so surprising that Jews don't want Gentile culture forced on them? Originally, Jewish culture was a stumbling block to Gentiles. Now the shoe is on the other foot. Will Gentiles respond with the same merciful flexibility? They will; they must: it is a historical imperative and nothing can stop it. The Scriptures declaring that all Israel shall be saved will be fulfilled.

Beyond merely permitting Gentiles freedom from Jewish customs and laws, Paul warned against anyone teaching Jews not to circumcise their children or keep the law of Moses (Acts 21:19-21).

If Paul thought the Five Books of Moses were destructive to Christianity, he would have said so. However, the entire book of Acts portrays Paul as a temple-loving Rabbi who performed circumcision and vows in the Temple and kept Jewish holidays with his fellow Jews. While he is pictured as accommodating the Gentiles, he was not hostile to his fellow Hebrews. As a matter of fact, Paul insisted that Timothy undergo circumcision in order that Timothy (a Jew) might win other Jews (Acts 16:3).

Simply because Jewish lifestyle is culturally foreign to non-Jews, is no reason to believe that the faith of Messianic Gentiles is more valid if it lacks Jewishness.

Non-Jewish believers themselves have something to learn about ceremonial freedom. Mainline Christian denominations have ceremonies that have little or no biblical basis. Who can say their church does not follow the same liturgical order week in and week out? What about the offertory and doxology? Aren't these ritualized procedures? Some non-biblical procedures have become so fixed that variance has caused many a church split. Take, for example, how denominations disagree over communion or baptismal rites. True freedom given to us in the New Covenant means having options for self-expression. The Lord looks at our hearts. As soon as someone says such ceremonies are forbidden, hasn't true freedom been diminished? Motivation is the key thing, and that is what the New Testament is all about.

For Gentiles, the Mosaic Law only had the implication of a heretical and futile effort to gain salvation. For Jewish people, the laws have the purpose of sustaining a valued culture. Traditional Jews of the modern age are not seeking salvation; they want to continue as a cohesive and identifiable group. The observance of Jewish traditions is important to them, since it provides a means of preserving themselves as a people. This is consistent with God's plan to preserve an identifiable group of Jewish people to inherit the promised land. This strong desire is deeply implanted. How then can believing Jews and Gentiles worship together?

We should look to the experience of those believers who lived 1,900 years ago. One should especially look at the advice laid down by James, an apostle to the Jews, and Paul, an apostle to the Gentiles. In brief, their advice was this: in a Gentile situation, Jews should not offend Gentiles by avoiding them, and in a Jewish setting Gentiles should be willing to accommodate Jewish customs (Acts 15: 19-20). This was consistent with Romans 14:13-15, which advises everyone to do what is pleasing to his brother, rather than to himself, in order to promote unity.

The Lord's plan was not exclusively for Jews, but for all mankind. He knew the weakness of human nature. He also foresaw that many of the Jewish people would succumb to spiritual pride for having been called the chosen people. Providence allowed this, since it permitted a time during which the Gentiles could spread the faith to the four corners of the earth. With Jews also in worldwide dispersion, the Almighty was laying the groundwork for the ultimate salvation of His ancient people.

Since Jews were so scattered, obviously it would take large numbers of preachers to explain His plan to them. After all, how were they to learn of the program except from people willing to preach? Since there are millions of true Gentile Christians, it seems reasonable that this could be accomplished within a single generation. Ultimately, the world's Jewish population will be reached primarily through the mercy of the Gentiles.

It is God's just plan for this to occur. The Scriptures

say we should not owe anything to anyone. This goes beyond financial debt. It means that if someone extends themselves we should endeavor to extend ourselves in return.

In financial terms, the Bible says the debtor is servant to the creditor. In a way, the believing Christian is indebted to the Jew. Unless Jews accomplished all that was recorded in the Old Covenant, the Gentile Christians would have no basis for their faith in the God of Israel. Gentile Christians also owe a debt of gratitude to Jewish apostles who suffered, bled and died to bring this good news to the world.

Not only in the apostolic era, but also in more recent times, the church has been enriched by the thoughts and labors of Jewish believers in the Messiah. While many churches have given their Jewish members a warm welcome, others have not made them feel at ease.

In some cases, a less than enthusiastic response has intensified the foreignness of the church to the new Jewish believer. This contributes to the natural desire of Jews to seek the companionship of others like themselves.

True Christians who feel that they owe something to Jews, will not discourage this activity. In fact, they can use their knowledge of Messianic Judaism to help bring Jewish people into a greater understanding of their own Bible.

When this occurs, Jews will owe a debt of gratitude to Christian believers. Then the books will be balanced. Jews brought God's Word to the Gentiles and the Gentiles will have returned it.

Beyond just understanding what makes Jewish people tick, the Scriptures show born-again Christians how to win the Jew. He is to provoke him to jealousy. This means showing Jews qualities of love and joy that they would want for themselves. In this way, God will accomplish His purpose, not by might or power, but by His Spirit.

As the peaceful spirit shows through the believers, they will wonder how they can obtain peace that passes understanding.

When the Jewish person is in so much difficulty that he is shopping for solutions and looking for supernatural intervention, he then will be open to the saving knowledge of the Messiah.

It has taken almost 2,000 years of dispersion to bring the Jewish people to the point where they were willing to listen to reason. It also has taken that long for the Jewish people to lose interest in meaningless ceremony. The lost sheep of the house of Israel are looking for the meaning of their lives. Now, Jews can have their cake and eat it, too. They are realizing that they don't have to become Gentiles in order to believe in Yeshua. When this realization occurs for an individual, it is no time for Gentiles to mess things up by creating needless obstacles. This is the time to emphasize the Jewishness of these concepts. It should be explained that it is not the Jew who converts to Christianity when he accepts this Jewish promise. It is the Gentile who converts to true Judaism when he accepts the Saviour. Since believing God is the basis of Biblical Judaism and since true Christianity is consistent with this, why not consider the New Testament to be Jewish? This is a valid approach when speaking to a Jewish person, especially since true Judaism predates Christianity.

What an honor to participate in the final hour of God's patient plan and to bring the good news to the ancient Hebrews. Unfortunately, there is too little interest in Jewish work. Is this because of ignorance, envy or jealousy? Is it the natural reaction of a sibling who sees his father's delight upon the return of the prodigal son? Is it because God called Israel the apple of His eye? No other nation in history has had God's guarantee of permanent existence.

In Genesis 12:3, God promised Abraham He would

"bless those who bless thee and curse them who curse thee." This eternal promise, given to Abraham and his seed stands despite all that has transpired through the centuries. Since the Jewish people cannot be destroyed, displaced or absorbed, they will be saved as Jews.

In effect, God has given the world an offer it can't refuse. It is a matter of the carrot or the stick. Yet the nations, over the centuries have chosen God's cursings by mistreating the Jewish people. The people who have done this either did not believe God or were too ignorant to choose blessings instead of cursings. Why not follow God's instructions on how to obtain blessings? He said he would bless those who bless the Jewish people. Christians should consider the selfishness of keeping this knowledge a secret. An almighty God who has freely given of Himself wants others to follow in the same path, to perform His will concerning Abraham's seed. The time is short.

XII
THE FUTURE OF ABRAHAM'S SEED

The Bible is an amazing book and has been so accurate in the past, it is only natural to contemplate what it says about the future.

As has been the case with all prophecies, they are best seen in retrospect. So the order of coming events is something of a mystery even to the most learned believers. Clearly, the peoples of the earth stand on the brink of some truly staggering events. Perhaps it is interesting to see how things develop for the State of Israel, the seed of Jacob, and for believers after the dust settles. If we knew more precisely the eventual end, it would be most helpful in interpreting present day events.

For almost 2,000 years many prophecies have remained unfulfilled. But suddenly Israel has its statehood. The ancient cities are being built up. The desert "blossoms as a rose." Jerusalem once again is under the control of the Jewish people. The Messiah said when the fig tree begins to blossom (Israel brought to life), mankind should look up for redemption draws near. The Psalms say "when the Lord builds up Zion (Israel), He shall appear in His glory."

It took a long time for these events to ripen. This is because the controversy between Jews and God has lasted for almost 20 centuries. Many Jewish people either deliberately ignore God, or are oblivious to His special purpose for them.

For all practical purposes, most of the Jewish people have severed contact with His Word which gives them their special place in history. The situation is similar to the days of King Saul, when Jewish people wanted a king so they could be like all the other nations. Israel today seeks a purely secular, political role in the world. It wants to be like all other nations.

Israel cannot imitate other nations. The spirit of anti-Semitism, if nothing else, has insured that. But there will not always be ill-feeling against the Jewish people. After Israel acknowledges her departure from God, she will assume her proper role among the nations. Moses records it this way:

> "... ye shall be a peculiar treasure unto me above all people for all the earth is mine; and ye shall be unto me a kingdom of priests and a holy nation..." (Exodus 19:5, 6).

> "When the most High divided to the nations their inheritance, when He separated the sons of Adam, He set the bounds of the people, according to the number of children of Israel, For the Lord's portion in his people; Jacob is the lot of his inheritance" (Deuteronomy 32:8,9).

> Isaiah also recorded: "This people I have formed myself; they shall tell of my praise" (Isaiah 43:21).

> "Thou art my servant, O Israel, in whom I will be glorified" (Isaiah 49:3).

> "Yet now hear, O Jacob my servant; and Israel, whom I have chosen" (Isaiah 44:1).

Other prophets are in similar record.

> "I have loved thee with an everlasting love; therefore with loving kindness have I drawn thee" (Jeremiah 31:3).

> "And I will betroth thee unto me for ever; yea, I will betroth thee unto me in righteousness, and in judgment, and in loving kindness, and in mercies. I will even betroth thee unto me in faithfulness: and thou shalt know the Lord" (Hosea 2:19,20).

> "And I will bring the third part through the fire, and will refine them as silver is refined, and will try them as gold is tried; they shall call on my name, and I will hear them: I will say, it is my people: and they shall say, the Lord is my God" (Zechariah 13:9).

> "And the heathen shall know that I the Lord do sanctify Israel, when my sanctuary shall be in the midst of them for evermore" (Ezekiel 37:28).

Who is the Lord's sanctuary?

> "And he shall be for a sanctuary: but for a stone of stumbling and a rock of offence to both houses of Israel" (Isaiah 8:14).

Yeshua is our refuge and our sanctuary. When the Messiah comes again, all nations shall recognize Israel's unique role. To accomplish His timeless objective, the Lord preserved a remnant according to His promise.

"Yet I will leave a remnant, that ye may have some escape the sword among the nations, when ye shall be scattered through the countries" (Ezekiel 6:8).

This remnant has endured and were the people of God's choice, the people who could worthily bear the name "Israel", or Prince of God.

The Prince of God has been on a wayward journey and has temporarily shed the princely crown. However, the high calling of the Jews is available to them, though they have abandoned it for many centuries. They have been deceived into believing Yeshua was against His own people.

The deceiver, Satan, is looking for assistance. He can get it from anyone who will help him keep the truth from the Jewish people. So far, Satan has been successful in this regard. He has spread the lie that accepting Yeshua makes Jews lose their rich heritage. This is because up to this time the church has been ignorant of why they were having so much trouble explaining their case to the Jewish people.

The last book of the Bible says that 144,000 people, 12,000 from each tribe of Israel, will evangelize the world. A remnant always has been preserved for this reason. If Satan can destroy the Jews, the world never can be evangelized in the final hour of this age. This is Satan's strategy that God will not permit. "He that keepeth Israel shall neither slumber nor sleep."

This is in keeping with Jeremiah's prophecy concerning the indestructibility of Israel.

"Thus saith the Lord, which giveth the sun for light by day, and the ordinances of the moon and of the stars for a light by night, which divideth the sea when the waves thereof roar; The Lord of hosts is his name: If those ordinances depart from before me, saith the Lord, then the seed of Israel also shall cease from being a nation before me for ever. Thus saith the Lord; If heaven alone can be measured, and the foundations of the earth searched out beneath, I will also cast off all the seed of Israel for all that they have done, saith the Lord" (Jeremiah 31:35-37).

What God has ordered, no force can undo.

Someday, Jacob's descendants not only will be called Jews, they will be Jews. The term Jews comes from Judah, or Yah-hooda, which means a "praiser of God." When Jews become praisers of God, then a new day will dawn. Here is how God says it will occur:

"For I will take you from among the heathens, and gather you out of all countries, and will bring you into your own land. Then will I sprinkle clean water upon you, and ye shall be clean: from all your filthiness, and from all idols, will I cleanse you. A new heart also will I give you, and a new spirit will I put within you: and I will give You a heart of flesh. And I will put my spirit within you, and cause you to walk in my statutes, and ye shall keep my judgments, and do them. And ye shall dwell in the land that I gave to your fathers; and ye shall be my people, and I will be your God" (Ezekiel 36:24-28).

One can see how God linked re-establishment of Israel as a nation to its spiritual awakening. There will be much suffering for Israel and the entire world before it is all over. In fact the Bible says there will be a terrible period for the Jews called the time of Jacob's trouble. All nations will be gathered against Jerusalem in battle, and two-thirds of the Jewish people will die. The surviving one-third will realize they will be completely annihilated unless they turn to God through the Messiah. Then they will accept Him as their Saviour and say, "blessed is He that comes in the name of the Lord."

> "And the Lord shall go forth and defend the inhabitants of Jerusalem ... and they shall look upon me whom they have pierced" (Zechariah 12:8, 10).

> "And one shall say unto him, What are these wounds in thine hands? Then he shall answer, Those with which I was wounded in the house of my friends" (Zechariah 13:6).

And when the Jewish people realize their mistake in rejecting Messiah the first time, there will be a great mourning in Jerusalem. The mourning shall be so great that every family shall want to be alone. And within each house, the wives will mourn separately from their husbands. At that time, the Jewish people will understand their own Scriptures. Jewish people know very little about the Bible today. The prophet Hosea says, "my people are destroyed for lack of knowledge." Amos says that in the last days there will be a famine, not of bread, but of the Word of God. Unfortunately, Jewish people are largely unaware of the significance of the prophecies being fulfilled today. This is about to change. Portions of the New Covenant now are required reading in many Israeli schools because of its authentic portrayal of first century Jewish history.

The Scriptures speak of a great calamity coming upon the earth. There are many nations mentioned as participants in a great war that surely will come. Let's look at three of them—Egypt, Israel and Russia.

One of the main participants in Israel's past difficulties, her present distress, and her future trouble is Egypt. Since

Egypt also is part of Abraham's progeny and plays so dominant a role in the future of Israel, it is important to see what
the Bible has to say about its past, present and future.
Egypt's history predates Israel's, and according to the Bible
the final chapters of this age will be written for both nations.

Before Babylon and Assyria built their empires, Egypt
had worldwide influence. This was due to the rich natural
resources of the Nile Valley and its Mediterranean Delta,
This fertile farmland made Egypt the breadbasket of the
Middle East. However, Egypt was morally corrupt and
served many false gods.

For centuries this land was inhabited by the descendents
of Ham (Noah's son) who settled on the African continent.
Like Israel, Egypt's spiritual heritage began with Abram
(later called Abraham) in about 2000 B.C. Sarai (later called
Sarah), Abram's wife, was more than 80 years old and Isaac
had not yet been born. In Genesis 16:2, Sarai said to Abram:

> "Behold now, the Lord hath restrained me from bear-
> ing: I pray thee, go in unto my maid; it may be that I
> may obtain children by her..."

Abram listened to Sarai's suggestion and followed her
plan. They decided to take matters into their own hands.
Hagar, Sarai's maid, conceived. When Hagar realized she
was going to have a child by Abram she developed contempt
for Sarai. Later, Sarai dealt harshly with Hagar and con-
vinced Abram to cast her out into the wilderness.

It was then that the Lord appeared to Hagar and made
her a promise concerning Ishmael her son, and his descendent. An angel of the Lord said:

> "...I will multiply thy seed exceedingly, that it shall
> not be numbered for multitude" (Genesis 16:10).

"He (Ishmael) will be a wild man; his hand will be against every man, and every man's hand against him; and he shall dwell in the presence of all his brethren" (Genesis 16:12).

It was determined that Ishmael's descendents (the Arab peoples) would be multiplied to the point where they could not be counted. The reference to his being a "wild man" describes his descendents as a free and roving people. For thousands of years this has permitted the Arab nations to keep their independence. These Scriptures also tell of the Arabs' propensity for war.

Abraham loved his son, Ishmael. He said, "Oh that Ishmael might live before thee" (Genesis 17:18). Abraham hoped that God wouldn't forget Ishmael. God knew this and in Genesis 17:20 the Lord made a promise concerning Ishmael: "I have blessed him, (Ishmael) and I will make him fruitful, and he will multiply exceedingly ... twelve princes shall he beget ... I will make him a great nation."

Although the promise of the covenant would be realized through Sarah's son, Isaac, Ishmael also was to be the father of a great people. The blessings of the Abramic covenant also were available to them. It can be seen that the Lord also had a special mission for Ishmael. When he and his mother, Hagar, were thirsting in the desert, having been cast out at Sarai's request, God said, "Arise, lift up the lad, and hold him in thine hand, for I will make of him a great nation" (Genesis 21:18).

Indeed Ishmael did have twelve sons which became the modern day Arab nations—Lebanon, Syria, Yemen, Iraq, Jordan, Saudi Arabia, Egypt, Sudan, Libya, Tunisia, Algeria and Morocco. Of these, Egypt has played the leading role.

But Egypt will not always be at odds with Israel. Isaiah speaks of a time when the Bible will be so well understood that Egypt and Israel will dwell together in peace and harmony.

"... And the Lord shall be known to Egypt, and the Egyptians shall know the Lord in that day, and shall do sacrifices and oblation; yea, they shall vow a vow unto the Lord, and perform it. And the Lord shall smite Egypt; he shall smite and heal it: and they shall return even to the Lord, and he shall be entreated of them, and shall heal them..."

"In that day shall Israel be the third with Egypt and with Assyria (the other Arab nations made up Assyria), even a blessing in the midst of the land; whom the Lord of hosts shall bless, saying, Blessed be Egypt my people, and Assyria the work of my hands, and Israel mine inheritance" (Isaiah 19:21-25).

Russia is another prominent character in Israel's future. She is going to be used to bring judgment on Israel and then she also will be judged. Being so large and so powerful a nation, it is important for Israel's allies to understand Soviet intentions.

We should not let wishful thinking cloud our understanding of the Lord's intent. Difficulties are in store for Israel so that the Jewish people will finally turn to Yeshua for help.

In the process, catastrophe will engulf Russia because it is blatantly against God, with atheism its accepted religion. Russia, therefore, is against the Bible which has to be smuggled into that country. Most of all, Russia will be judged because it is against Israel.

In Ezekiel 38:3 God says, "I am against thee, O Gog, the chief prince of Meshech and Tubal." Prophetic scholars pretty much agree which ancient tribes these names refer to, and in what area they settled. Meshech refers to a tribe which settled near what has become Moscow. Tubal refers to the city of Tobolsk on the Tobol River.

The Russian leaders will think an evil thought against Israel (Ezekiel 38:10). Russia will come like a storm and like a cloud to cover the land (Ezekiel 38:9,16). Already one can see the handwriting on the wall. Russia is determined to get an easier access to the Mediterranean Sea. Most of all, it wants to control the Middle East and its oil.

The Bible does not give us an exact time when this will occur. It does, however, give us some clues. According to Ezekiel 38:16, it will happen in the "latter years."

Concerning Israel's ultimate destiny, the Bible says:

"And he shall judge among the nations, and shall rebuke many people: and they shall beat their swords into plowshares, and their spears into pruning hooks: nation shall not lift up sword against nation, neither shall they learn war any more" (Isaiah 2:4).

"The wolf also will dwell with the lamb, and the leopard shall lie down with the kid; and the calf and the young lion and the fatling together; and a little child shall lead them. And the cow and the bear shall feed; their young ones shall lie down together: and the lion shall eat straw like the ox. And the suckling child shall play on the hole of the asp, and the weaned child shall put his hand on the basilisk's den. They shall not hurt nor destroy in all my holy mountain: for the earth shall be full of the knowledge of the Lord, as the waters cover the sea" (Isaiah 11:6-9).

Note that this prophecy will come to pass when the earth is full of knowledge of the Lord. No world leader who undermines God's Word or His almighty power ever can lead anyone to true peace.

Isaiah goes on to say when these events come to pass, a descendent of Jesse (Yeshua) will stand as a sign to the nations, and that the nations will seek Him. Then things shall be restored to the way God intended them from the beginning. God's peace will cover the earth and all mankind shall be filled with the knowledge of Him.

EPILOGUE

It has been over 25 years since this book was first written. During that time the Messianic Movement has thrived. Jewish people who believe the Messiah has come can no longer be dismissed as individual lunatics.

At this writing well over tens of thousands of Jewish people around the world have found their Messiah. Often times significant numbers accept Yeshua and band together without any knowledge that this is also occurring elsewhere. Today, Jewish believers can be found not only in the United States, but also in Canada, England, France, Australia, Russia, Chile, Colombia, Belgium, Germany, Switzerland, Holland, Argentina, Uraguay, South Africa, Brazil, New Zealand, Portugal, Mexico, Israel and countries of the former Soviet Union.

In the U.S. there are now some 250 functioning Messianic groups at various stages of development. In Israel, there are approximately 70 groups which meet for worship and study.

This compares favorably with 30 years ago when these were only a few. Can this rapid rise be explained by human effort alone? How can this growth be rationalized in the face of dwindling synagogue attendance by Jewish people of more traditional affiliations? The answer is that Messianic congregations and synagogues are able to satisfy deep inner needs. Today's society tends to be skeptical and less bound by social pressures to conform to the past. As the population has grown more mobile and urban, it has also produced a degree of anonymity and sense of alienation. Thus, religion in the usual sense won't do. People don't want rituals and empty words. They are looking for explanations which will help them get through life better.

Human beings were created with a built in need to relate to their creator. The Bible says that Jewish people have a zeal for God. Just because some ancient ancestors made some unfortunate errors, is no reason why Jewish people cannot go back to their roots and reclaim their personal relationship with the God of Abraham, Isaac and Jacob. This is what will bring satisfaction and joy.

BIBLIOGRAPHY

Brotman, Manny. Training Brochure on "How to Share Messiah." Washington, D.C.: Messianic Jewish Movement International, 1972.

Brotman, Manny. The Jewish Bible Approach. Washington, D.C.: Messianic Jewish Movement International, 1972.

Duncan, Homer. Israel: Past, Present and Future. Lubbock, Texas: Missionary Crusader.

Finklestein, Joseph. Jewish Holidays, A Study Guide. Washington, D.C.: Messianic Jewish Movement International.

Fruchtenbaum, Arnold G. Hebrew Christianity: Its Theology, History and Philosophy. Washington, D.C.: Cannon Press, 1974.

Fruchtenbaum, Arnold G. Messianic Jewish History (Lectures at "Messiah '75" Conference, Messianic Jewish Alliance of America). Portsmouth, Virginia: Flow of Life Ministries, 1975.

Goble, Phil. "The Messianic Synagogue Movement: Is It Biblical?" (Essay). South Pasadena, California, 1975.

Goldberg, Dr. Louis. "The Messianic Jew." Jewish Voice, June and July, 1975.

Harkavy, Alexander. The Holy Scriptures. New York: Hebrew Publishing Co., 1936.

Huffman, Jean. "Sayings of Jesus and Their Hebraic Roots." Concern. May-June, 1973.

Kac, Arthur W. "Jewish Opposition to the Messianic Movement of Jesus." The American Hebrew Christian, Numbers 3 and 4, 1973.

Kirban, Salem. God Promises. Huntingdon Valley, Pennsylvania: Salem Kirban, Inc., 1971.

Meldau, Fred John. Messiah In Both Testaments. Denver, Colorado: The Christian Victory Publishing Co., 1956.

Moody Bible Institute Correspondence Course, Part I & II. "Shadow of the Almighty," "The Voice of God." Chicago, Illinois.

The New, Testament with Old Testament References. Philadelphia, Pennsylvania. Million Testaments Campaign.